TITL

Author, publisher, and seller assume no liabilities whatsoever. Sold as information only. Use caution with eye and skin protection when using tools or working on vehicles, engines, fuel, electricity, lubricating and cleaning fluids, etc.

How To Change The Oil On Your Twin Cam Motorcycle – Harley Davidson

A guide on how to change the three oil compartments on the motorcycle. Also cleaning or replacing the air filter and spark plugs with very important engine longevity advice.

Copyright by James Russell. All rights reserved. No part of this publication may be reproduced in any form or by any means without prior written permission of the author or publisher.

How To Change The Oil On Your Twin Cam Motorcycle – Harley Davidson

Printed in the United States of America.
Published by James Russell Publishing.com
Publisher SAN Number: 295-852X

How To Change The Oil On Your Twin Cam Motorcycle – Harley Davidson

Written by James Russell © January 2006.
Illustrations & Photos by James Russell
First Printed Edition © 2006 All Rights Reserved

BISAC Subject Heading: Number TRA003030 Motorcycles/ Repair & Maintenance

ISBN-10 No. 0-916367-75-4
ISBN-13 No. 978-0-916367-75-6

This book may be purchased from any bookstore or go to:
JamesRussellPublishing.com.

DEDICATED TO:

The Following Bible Quotes That Can Be Applied to Bikers

....

"He made him ride on the high places of the earth..." Leveticus 15 32:13 KJV

&

"For ye shall go out with joy, and be led forth with peace: the mountains and the hills shall break forth before you into singing, and all the trees of the field shall clap their hands."
II Kings 11 55:12 KJV

&

"And call upon me in the day of trouble: I will deliver thee..." Psalm 50:15 KJV

&

"Whosoever shall call upon the name of the Lord shall be saved."
Romans 10:13 KJV

....

TABLE OF CONTENTS

PREFACE

EASY TO CHANGE OIL & FILTER?

It is so easy a girl can do it. Just follow these easy step-by-step instructions. It requires no physical strength and you don't need to lift the bike onto a lift or a jack. We will the entire job with the bike resting on its side-stand

You will learn how to change the three engine oil compartments, replace the oil filter the air filter and the spark plugs. You will not require the assistance of anyone else to help you. Don't worry if you have never done it before. We will show you how easy it is to do!

You will learn a lot more than just how to change the oil and filter! Tips on how to make your engine last a lot longer and remain strong and powerful than it would otherwise is here inside this book.

Yes, even tips to give you more horsepower and fuel mileage.

READ THIS SAFETY CHAPTER FIRST

If you are new to performing maintenance work on motorcycles make sure you wear safety goggles so hot oil will not accidentally spray into your eyes. Never force any tools to perform beyond their capabilities. When pushing or pulling on a wrench expect that it will suddenly let loose. If you are prepared for this rapid loosening you will not skin your knuckles. Clean up any spilled oil right away so you or anyone else will not slip and fall down. Keep the motorcycle leaning on the bike's side stand. Do not use a lift to perform the maintenance described in this book, unless you have experience with such lifts and know of their dangers. A lift is not required at all and it is not recommended.

Take your time. Never be in a hurry and enjoy yourself. If things don't work out for you by making a mistake, don't worry about it or become upset. Stay calm and be safe. We all spill things and make mistakes. It‘s no big thing. If you have any safety concerns just speak with your local Harley Davidson dealer’s mechanic. They can give you sound advice and let you read the service manual.

In fact, it is a good idea to just buy a service manual. It will not give you every procedure in step-by-step detail as this book gives, but it will expand your knowledge so you can expand your maintenance and repair capabilities.

Did you know that many motorcycle mechanics actually began their career by learning how to change the oil on their own motorcycles then they did the job on their friend’s bikes and then were hired by a motorcycle dealer. See *Cuts and Scrapes* in the *Helpful Advice* section.

READ THIS CHAPTER SECOND

What is new is the Perpetual Oil Change chapter you should check out right away before you change your oil the conventional way. If you have recently changed your oil you should begin to use this oil sweetening method between major scheduled oil changes. Why? Because your engine will be running on new, fresh and cleaner oil all of the time and that means more power and engine longevity for you that will save you a lot of money. You will save so much money it will easily pay for the cost of this book many, many times over. Actually, thousands of dollars in savings!

Go to the Perpetual Oil Change chapter right now. Read and learn about this revolutionary new technique successfully proven and developed by James Russell for the motorcycle industry.

OIL CHANGE & FILTER FREQUENCY

Your Harley Davidson dealer and the owner manual is your best guide as they will have any new recommendation updates that should be followed. As of this writing:

- Engine oil & oil filter– change at each 2,500 miles.
- Primary oil – change at each 5,000 miles.
- Transmission oil – change at each 5,000 miles.
- Air filter – clean or replace each 10,000 miles.
- Spark plugs – check at each 5,000 miles or replace each 10,000 miles.

We will explain how to use synthetic oils and mixing oil blends in this book as we go along.

Tools: I have shown the tools you will need in the photos and in callout item lists. You should buy the 3/8" size sockets and drives for oil changing. The big heavy ½" drives and sockets are overkill and sometimes just get in the way of getting the job performed quickly as they are too thick in size to get into tight spaces.

Sockets: If you can buy 12-point sockets, then do so. You will need them to work on the brake calipers and some other engine areas. However, if all you are going to do is oil changing then the 6-point sockets will be just fine.

Buying Tools: you do not need to buy expensive tools for this job. If pride of having the best tools is your thing (it is with me) then Craftsman Tools by Sears is still one of the best buy. Some mechanics like Snap On Tools. Sears has a good lifetime warrantee (on most all hand tools with rare exceptions) and they feel good in the hand when using them. You can buy a huge set of tools at discount, but it is actually wiser to just buy the minimum tools you will need to fix your Harley Davidson motorcycle. At this point, we are just keeping the costs down low so you can buy just the tools you need to change the oils, oil filter, air filter and spark plugs. Many people do not want to perform other repairs, they only want to do their own oil, plug and filter changes and that is what we focus on in this book.

This way you will have all the tools and parts you will need all packed into a nice small toolbox and it will save you a bundle of cash. It makes life so much easier this way. I learned this the hard way. You do not need a huge tool-chest full of expensive tools. Just buy what you need to get the job done and you will no longer have to search through dozens of tools just to find the one tool you need. This only slows the job down and frustrates you on top of it.

Cuts & Scrapes: It happens to all of us. We will cut or scrape a finger or knuckle. Wash the cut with soap and water, apply some anti-biotic ointment then use liquid band aid or a standard band aid. If you work slowly and at ease the odds are you will have no mishaps. It is when you rush a job such accidents happen. Relax and enjoy yourself. This is supposed to be fun, right?

Motorcycle Lift of Jack: None is required. We will perform the entire job with the bike leaning on its normal side kickstand. You will not even need the assistance of another person to help you.

WHY DO IT YOURSELF?

Save Money: performing your own oil change is not only cost effective, but you will know it is being performed right and the proper oils are being added to your engine. You will save more than money as you employ the engine longevity tips I have given in this book and some performance increase tips you may employ to squeak about five to six more horsepower.

You Ride a Lot: if you are like me who travels extensively putting on over 22,000 miles a year you need to perform your own oil changes to save money and time. Sometimes dealers are not available and you don't want to spend time or money to do such simple work. As a mechanic, I can't fathom paying to have my bike's oil changed when I can do it myself in half the time and half the cost.

No Waiting: You don't need to leave your bike in a repair shop waiting for it to be serviced. You just wake up and get the job done at home in less than one hour and away you go.

Engine Wear: you can prevent heavy engine wear. If a mechanic does not prime the oil filter with oil the engine will run dry of oil upon starting. You can actually hear metal-to-metal contact tearing up the engine for a few seconds. Not good! When you change your own oil you know this will not happen to your bike.

Increase Fuel Mileage: when you change the oil you can add additives a dealer will not normally add to your engine to reduce friction and heat that will increase your fuel mileage, horsepower and engine life.

Safety is also another good reason: When you do it yourself you know everything is snug and proper. If a mechanic forgets to tighten the oil drain plug on the engine, primary case or transmission or overfills the oil tank oil can spill out to the rear wheel and cause a horrific crash. Accidents happen. When you do it yourself you know it is going to be done right the first time.

DO IT YOURSELF

You need not have to wait anymore for an oil change. Just step outside and do it yourself. It is easy once you know how... this book teaches you how easy it is!

THIS BOOK CAN MAKE YOU MONEY

You can make money in your spare time performing oil changes for your friends. This will help you earn money to buy a new Harley Davidson motorcycle or to buy optional equipment you have always wanted but could not afford. Think about that! Maybe the Harley dealer could use your help changing oil on bikes for them in their shop when times are busy for them, especially during motorcycle rally events. As you can see, this book can even launch you into a motorcycle mechanic career!

SPARE PARTS FOR YOUR HOME TOOLBOX

There are some minor spare parts you should have on hand. As you are working you may lose one or find it is worn down and needs replacement on the spot. This way you will have a spare and not have to go to the dealer to get a part, interrupting your oil change job. These parts are for your home toolbox not for your motorcycle toolkit.

1. Oil drain o-rings – get a dozen. One size fits all oil drain plugs.
2. Primary Case inspection gasket.
3. Oil drain plug for Primary Chain Case.
4. Teflon paste and Teflon tape.
5. Oil drain plug for engine oil (can be used for transmission).
6. Air cleaner screw (one of three that holds the air cleaner on throttle-body).

NO SPOKES

Did you know that if you get a flat tire with a spoke-wheel it can not be fixed by a tow truck driver or at a nearby auto repair shop? You need tire-irons, a tube and/or a patch kit. Tubeless tires can be plugged like a car tire to get you down the road again right away. That means you need a bike with cast wheels, not a bike with spokes.

CHAPTER 1

AIR FILTER CHANGE / CLEANING

First, before we change the oil we will clean or replace the air filter. But before we do anything:

LOCK THE IGNITION SWITCH INTO THE OFF POSITION SO NOBODY CAN START THE BIKE BUT YOU.

If others have a key, then place a tag on the handlebar that says:

DO NOT START ENGINE – I AM WORKING ON THE MOTOR.

You can also disconnect the negative battery terminal that way the bike can't be started by anyone.

BATTERY TIPS

When disconnecting a battery terminal make sure your wrench does not contact any metal. You can wrap the wrench handle in electrical tape or cloth. After the terminal is free place a cloth rag around the wire's end terminal so it will not slowly gravitate to contact metal. It will often return to the battery terminal without you noticing it or touch the bike's metal frame. You can also tape it into place so it will not relocate.

When replacing an old battery do a little investigative work as many new aftermarket batteries are inferior and sold at a low price and some retailers may actually sell these low quality batteries at a high price to mimic the better batteries. Try to replace the battery with the same model Harley Davidson uses or purchase a trusted well-known aftermarket brand with a good warrantee.

Fig. 1 Removing Air Cleaner Cover

Use the 5/16" Allen wrench to remove the chrome air cleaner cover. Turn the wrench counterclockwise to loosen.

Turn the cover over and use it to store the screws and Allen wrenches so they do not get lost. See Fig. 2. At Sears and at most auto parts stores you can buy a magnetic bowl or a magnetic mat to hold all your nuts, bolts, screws and tools. It works real nice as they prevent items from getting lost.

TOOL BUYING TIP

You can go to Sears or another tool supplier and just buy the individual tool you need instead of having to buy the entire set of tools. We call out the tool required in this book to make it easier for you to do this.

Unless you plan on performing many repairs there is really no reason to have complete sets of tools for the person who just wants to change the oil in their own motorcycle.

Fig. 2 Use Air Cleaner Cover to Store Tool and Screws

The air cleaner is shown in Fig. 3 and is held in place with three screws. Two have already been removed while the third is removed using a 5/32" Allen wrench.

AIR FILTER ELEMENT

The aftermarket high performance type air filter elements are generally of much higher expectations than factory stock when it comes to higher rates of air flow. It is recommended that you stay with the original Harley Davidson brand of air filter element because it is configured to your stock engine. Altering air flow rates can create lean fuel burning that will damage the pistons and valves in your engine.

Fig. 3 Removing Air Cleaner Element With Allan Wrench

Insert the Allan wrench and turn the screw counterclockwise. There are three screws to remove that fastens the air cleaner.

DYNA, SPORTSTER AND OTHER MODELS

This book can easily be used to change the oil on most all Harley Davidsons as the procedure is much the same. Just find the location of the oil drain plugs, the type of oil and o-rings you need to use.

The tools and procedure may need to be altered a bit, but once you have done it the first time you can write reminder notes in this book's margins to identify any major differences.

Fig. 4 Removing Engine Air Filter

The filter is easily removed to replace or be cleaned and oiled as is the case with this filter being a K&N high performance reusable filter. See Fig. 4, 5 and 6.

CLEANING TIPS

Do not use harsh chemical or automotive-type cleaning products on your motorcycle such as "brake cleaner" as it can damage o-rings and seals even on your brake calipers! It can also stain paint and seriously erode coatings that protect engine and frame finish.

Just use dishwashing detergent and water for the cleaning needed for performing oil changes. You can use cleaning products your Harley Davidson dealer provides.

Fig. 5 Applying Degreaser Fluid

K&N makes a cleaning solution to clean the filter. Here in Fig. 5 we have sprayed the solution on the filter media and in Fig. 6 we are now washing it off with hot water.

Note: After washing the air filter element you need to let it dry out by gently blowing it out with compressed air or set it into the air stream of a fan until dry so the oil to be sprayed on the filter medium will adhere.

Note: Harley Davidson stock bikes will have disposable filter elements. Just install the new filter. Do not apply oil or wash the filter as with the K&N filter shown. Buy your filter from your Harley Davidson dealer.

Note: You can buy and install a reusable high-flowing air filter element (like the K&N type) and it will not increase air flow in the engine to lean it out, as long as your stock exhaust pipes are installed. See your Harley Davidson dealership for professional advice before making any alterations to your motorcycle.

Fig. 6 Washing the Air Filter

Note that we are washing the filter from the inside so the water flows from the inside to the outside of the filter. This process works best to flush out grime.

Examine the filter and look to see if the pleats are indeed clean. Often, dried bugs and grease will be found deeply inside the exterior portion of the pleats in the filter media. Use a small toothpick to remove this hidden grime so the air cleaner will be 100% perfectly clean.

Let the air filter air dry or gently blow the residual water out. In any case the filter should be dry before you oil it. Apply the oil liberally so the filter media turns red (the color of the filter oil). The oil is sprayed from the inside and on the outside of the filter media.

Wipe off the excess oil and install the filter back on the bike.

To reinstall just reverse the process. Do not over tighten the screws. You can place a drop of removable thread-locking compound on the screws if you wish, but it is not required. I like to use aluminum base anti-seize thread compound so they will not rust into place and will make removal easier. See Fig. 61 showing a silver tube of Permatex brand aluminum base anti-seize compound.

Just tighten the screws until they are snug. See Fig. 7 and Fig. 8.

To reinstall just reverse the process. Do not over-tighten the screws. You can place a drop of removable thread-locking compound on the screws if you wish, but it is not required. I like to use aluminum base anti-seize thread compound so they will not rust into place and will make removal easier. See Fig. 61 showing a silver tube of Permatex brand aluminum base anti-seize compound.

Just tighten the screws until they are snug. See Fig. 7 and Fig. 8.

You will need to turn the air filter element so all three screw holes on the intake manifold will line up with the filter element. Just turn the filter left or right. When all three holes appear to line up then insert the screws and tighten as shown. Just snug the screws so you do not strip the head or threads.

Fig. 7 Tightening Air Filter Screws

Note: Thread-locking compounds generally come in two basic colors. Blue is removable so that is the color you would want to use on any motorcycle component. Red compounds are usually used for critical internal engine parts as removal of the red compound is very difficult and can require a blow torch, so only use blue.

Fig. 8 Replacing Air Filter Cover

This job is now finished.

How often should the air cleaner be cleaned? Not as often as you think. It can be replaced or cleaned every six months regardless of mileage. Of course, if you want to clean the filter at each oil change that is up to you.

CHAPTER 2

ENGINE OIL CHANGE

Engine Oil Change

Must engine be hot? Yes, due to oil will drain into the crankcase sump when the engine cools down. Also hot oil retains contaminates so they can be removed. The primary and transmission oil can be changed when the oil is cold. So, take the bike for a short ride (even if it is just around the block) then let's drain the engine oil.

Fig. 9 Tools & Parts to Change Engine Oil

This is the right-hand side of the bike in Fig. 10 showing the location of the oil drain plug. It will be found recessed inside the bike's frame. Yes, a bit hidden from view and hard to locate if this is your first time.

Use the 5/8" socket and turn the drain plug counterclockwise to loosen.

Caution: be ready for the drain plug to suddenly break free so you don't skin your knuckles.

That is why we use an extension on the wrench. Note that we have now placed the oil drain pan to catch the oil.

The tools we will use are in the oil drain pan as shown in Fig. 9.

1. Tube of liquid Teflon pipe thread sealant.
2. Oil drain plug o-ring (obtain from Harley Davidson dealer).
3. Oil filer wrench with cut-out slot (obtain from Harley Davidson dealer).
4. 5/8" Socket
5. 3" socket extension.
6. Socket wrench.
7. Plastic kitty litter pan to catch the drained oil.

Fig. 10 Removing Engine Oil Drain Nut

Helpful Tip: seeing a fine dust of aluminum or steel in drained engine oil is not too much of a problem as long as there is only a very small amount, for example; less than a wet fingertip touching grains of fine salt. Any more than this? Show it to your Harley Davidson dealer. Any visible amount of brass or bronze is a problem and needs to be addressed.

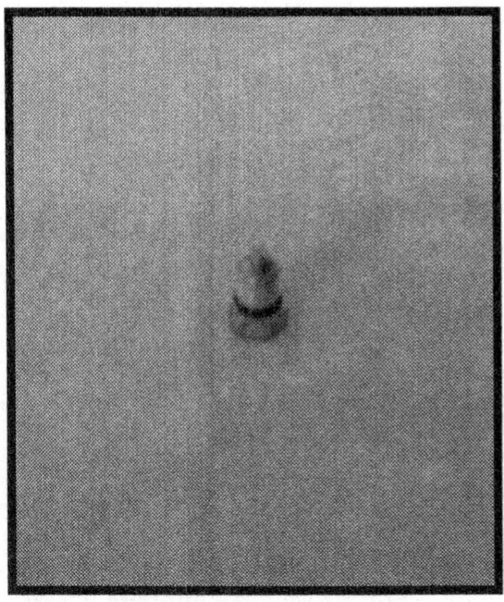

Fig. 11 Oil Drain Plug

This is what the oil drain plug looks like. In Fig. 11 we have applied a new rubber o-ring and coated the threads with liquid Teflon plumbers paste in Fig. 12. If the o-ring were to fail the Teflon will hold the oil very well inside the engine and it makes removal of the plug easier. Just apply a thin coat of Teflon to the threads. Enough to fill the threads is all that is required. It does not matter if Teflon is applied to the rubber O-ring or not.

You don't absolutely need to use Teflon on this oil drain, but it is a good product to use. Can you use Teflon tape? Yes, you can but the paste works best for this service as it will not interfere with the o-ring or reduce bolt penetration depth.

On the tip of the bolt is a magnet. Yes, you will often find some fine metal magnetic filings on the magnet. Just wipe them away and don't worry about it. In most cases it is just common metal wear. This is normal.

Fig. 12 Teflon Plumbers Paste

Fig. 12 (and Fig. 38) reveals the Teflon pipe joint compound. You will use this non-hardening paste on other drain plugs on your bike. You can buy it at any hardware store.

You must use a new o-ring each time you remove this drain plug. The threads scratch and cut the o-ring the moment you install it, so never reuse the o-ring.

Buy a dozen of these o-rings so you will have them on hand. They can easily become lost and you will need them for the transmission oil drain plug too.

Note: The engine oil and the transmission oil drain plugs are identical and both use the same size o-ring (unless a design change has taken place). You should have a spare oil drain plug on hand just in case you lose one.

Fig. 13 Transmission Oil Drain Plug

If you look at the oil drain nut you will notice there is an Allen bolt hole on the nut side. Do not use an Allen wrench on this oil drain plug because it will only strip if you try to loosen it and if you try to tighten the nut with an Allen it will not get tight and will leak oil. Keep reading for more instructions when to use the Allen wrench on this drain bolt.

In Fig. 13 we show the wrench is applied ready to tighten, but you need to hold the socket extension with your left hand so the socket will not slip off the nut. Any time you use an extension on a socket you must do this, especially when servicing spark plugs.

Note: We need to talk about tightening o-ring sealed bolts because they feel different when they tighten than ordinary threaded bolts. You will notice as you tighten the oil drain bolt it will increasingly feel snug. You may be tempted to stop tightening the bolt thinking it is like a spark plug's crush washer compressing.

You need to keep on tightening the nut past this friction until the wrench will not move any more. The nut must be a tight fit. Just keep on turning that wrench until it stops and can't be moved. You will feel it bottom out against metal to metal very abruptly.

Note: do not be overly concerned about stripping bolt threads and not properly tightening oil drain plugs. You will likely have no trouble here, but I go into the finer details so you can "feel" and "understand" how the job is properly performed and so you will instantly know that something is not right when you "feel" it is not right. This way you can stop right away and this will prevent you from doing something you should not be doing. Even good mechanics sometimes make mistakes and strip a bolt hole. It is rare, but mistakes happen.

Caution: This oil drain nut must be tight or it can leak oil on the rear tire causing the bike to crash. Just make sure the nut stops turning as you apply strong wrench pressure. Once the nut stops, don't try to over-tighten the nut as you may strip the head of the nut off making removal the next time very difficult. You can use a torque wrench if you wish, but it usually is not necessary.

Now that you are aware of the different feel of these o-ring oil drain bolts you will have no problem with them. The novice will have problems as the nuts do tend to feel that they are snug tight, but if you apply a bit more wrench pressure you discover they keep on rotating. This means the oil drain plug is not tight. It is just the rubber o-ring creating friction giving a false feeling of tightness. You will know when the bolt is tight as it will simply stop tightening and lock-up as it binds on metal to metal contact. The wrench simply will not turn the bolt anymore.

MOTOR OIL

Many articles have been written about motor oils and still there is much confusion to this complex subject. Make life easy on yourself and just use the oil the manufacturer recommends you to us. Problem solved!

Fig. 14 Oil Tank / Oil Bag

This is the engine oil fill in the external oil tank. Some bikers call it the oil bag (I think it was rednecks that started this nonsensical name-calling). The oil dipstick is removed and sitting on the edge in Fig. 14. We will now add oil to the oil bag.

Fig. 15 Adding Oil to Oil Bag / Oil Tank

Here we are adding Harley Davidson's SYN3 Synthetic Lubricant to the oil bag. It is expensive, but it is very good oil and will absolutely increase the life of your engine and give you a couple horsepower increase. Some bikes will even get up to 5 horses.

Blending Oil: The synthetic oil is a bit too expensive to use for many bike owners, so it is okay to blend the engine oil. Just add one quart of Harley Davidson SYN3 synthetic and use the normal Harley Davidson 20-50 engine oil at each oil change.

Must you use Harley Davidson oil? Certainly not. As long as the oil API specs match the motorcycle manufacturers specs it is good to use. But, it is always wise to take the extra measure of caution and use the manufacturers' brand of oil. Why? Because they often have special additives added that can be beneficial to the engine seals and other components specific to the motorcycle.

....

HOW TO BUY A CRUISER MOTORCYCLE

Wouldn't it be neat to have a list that would guide you into getting not only the right motorcycle and the proper optional equipment to match, but also the best deal you could possibly get?

Well, we have such a list on our Website and it is "free." This list will help you to get the best deal and will guide you to ask the salesperson the right questions before you buy.

Many people make terrible mistakes when buying a motorcycle only to later regret the purchase. Use our free list *"How To Buy A V-Twin Cruiser Motorcycle"* and you will buy with confidence and complete peace of mind.

Go online to: JamesRussellPublishing.com

Can you mix different brands of oil? Yes, as long as the oil API specs match the motorcycle manufacturers' specs or exceed it. You could use Mobile 1 V-Twin 20-50 oil with Harley Davidson's synthetic and standard engine oil. I have done so many times never with any problems whatsoever. The API specs are on the oil container. In fact, a blend of ordinary oil with synthetic oil gives better wear protection than just using ordinary oil, by far. The blended oil will not break down in the heat as it is mixed with synthetic oil that can not break down. Do use blended oil if you want increased wear protection.

If you have never used synthetic oil in your twin cam engine before, go ahead and make the switch now. The synthetic oil is good oil and your engine is designed to handle these modern oils. Older bike engine designs like the Pan Head, shovel, knuckle, EVO should stay with ordinary oils, but you can add ¼ quart of synthetic to give you a protective edge. See the oil additive section in this book for more protection.

To add oil, just put in a quart first then add ¼ quart each time you check the oil with the dip stick. Make sure the bike is level, so sit on the bike when dipping the dipstick.

Note: you can level the bike by putting blocks of wood under the kickstand, but be careful the bike does not get pushed over by wind or accidentally bumped by a person or pet. The bike will then fall over.

Yes, the dipstick is pressed all the way down each time and then removed to check the oil level (read your owner manual or the instructions if you are using a custom dip stick). When the oil is on the lower mark it is okay. Do not fill it above the top-level mark so you will not overfill it.

More oil is not good – some believe that adding more oil is better, but it is actually harmful. It creates fuel-robbing and performance reducing drag on the engine and can actually damage piston rings in very severe overfilling of the engine cases. Do not fill the engine with oil above the dip stick "full" mark after the engine is started up after the oil change.

Do Not Disturb: When adding engine oil, do not answer the phone or become distracted. You must perform this procedure in one shot. If you were to add a quart of oil and then come back later the oil would have disappeared, slowly drained into the crankcase. Then you would come back and add oil to the fill mark on the dipstick. When you start the engine (after we change the oil filter) that extra quart of oil is going to come back to haunt you. It will make a horrible mess overflowing from the oil tank and could even wet your back tire and cause you to crash. It could even cause catastrophic engine damage if a hydraulic situation develops. Pay attention when adding oil!

Fig. 16 Adding Ordinary Engine Oil

We are now blending the oil with the Harley Davidson's original 20-50 oil in Fig. 16.

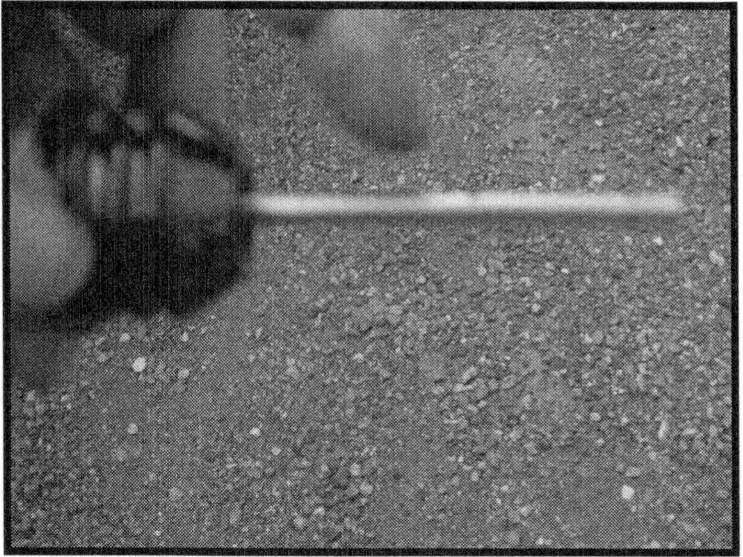

Fig. 17. The Engine Oil Dip Stick

Keep adding oil and checking the level (check the oil level with bike being level when you are sitting on the bike. Do not check the oil level with the bike leaning on the side kickstand). Stop when the oil reaches the lower mark. See Fig 17. The lower mark would be on the right side tip as shown in the photo.

Overfilling: if you accidentally fill it to the top level of the dipstick mark, it is still okay at this point, so don't worry about it. The oil level will drop again when we later change the oil filter. See the engine oil filter change section on how to fix overfilling the oil tank.

DIP STICK ADVICE

You would think it be safe to buy another type of dip stick and it usually is, but there are changes in procedure that needs to be adhered to, as some require the bike to be level, others do not. Some require the dip stick be inserted all the way into the oil tank, others do not. Make sure you get it right.

Fig. 18 Disposable Shop Towels

Here we have a most handy item; shop towels. I really like these Scott brand cloth rags on a roll. They are tough and absorb oil like a magnet. You can buy them at most automotive parts stores and at major department stores. You will need at least ½ roll to wipe up all the oil mess, mostly when cleaning the oil drain pan.

DISPOSING THE USED OIL

We now need to dispose the old engine oil. You can do this step last after you have changed the engine oil, oil filter, primary case and the transmission. All of these oils will not overflow the oil drain pan. However, it will not hurt to get a little bit of practice in with a little bit of oil on the first try. It can get very messy if you make a mistake with a full oil drain pan.

Fig. 19 Shop Towel Covering Sink Drain

As shown in Fig. 19 place two or three sheets of the absorbent cloth over the drain of your kitchen sink. This will prevent spilled oil going down the drain. Yes, you will spill oil in this procedure.

Fig. 19 shows only one shop towel. Since this will be your first time and you will likely spill oil, place a half-dozen sheets of shop towls in the sink to catch the oil.

Note: Oil flows slowly at first then it quickly tends to gush out at rapid speed. So when pouring... pour very slowly. It is not like pouring water.

Fig. 20 Draining Old Oil into Oil Container

You should use a funnel to pour oil from the drain pan to an empty oil container. But if you are a professional (like me) you can do it freehand as shown in Fig. 20. Be careful as the oil container fills rapidly and overflows fast making a huge spilling mess.

When you have finished filling the old oil containers mark them with a magic marker "OLD OIL" so you will not use them again. Take them to where you bought the oil and ask them to recycle the old oil. The oil cartel does not like this, but it is the right thing to do.

Note: If you are tempted to throw the oil into a trash dumpster don't do it. That oil will be wasted and can never be used by anyone ever again. The new oil you just used could have been recycled oil (oil never wears out, it just gets dirty). Please take the extra effort to recycle the oil.

Now, let's go change the engine oil filter.

CHAPTER 3

ENGINE OIL FILTER CHANGE

Fig. 21 Engine Oil Filter Tools & Supplies

These are the items you will need to change the engine oil filter. See Fig. 21.

1. Engine oil (Harley Davidson standard 20-50 weight or snythetic oil).
2. New oil filter with new o-ring.
3. Special slotted oil filter socket (purchase at Harley Davidson dealer).
4. 3" socket wrench extension.
5. 3/8" ratchet socket wrench.
6. Battery squeeze bulb – not shown in photo but see Fig. 31.

PRIMING THE OIL FILTER

The first thing we are going to do is prime that new oil filter. Position it as shown in Fig. 21 and add engine oil to that large center hole. Fill it to the top until it overflows into the smaller holes. See Fig. 22.

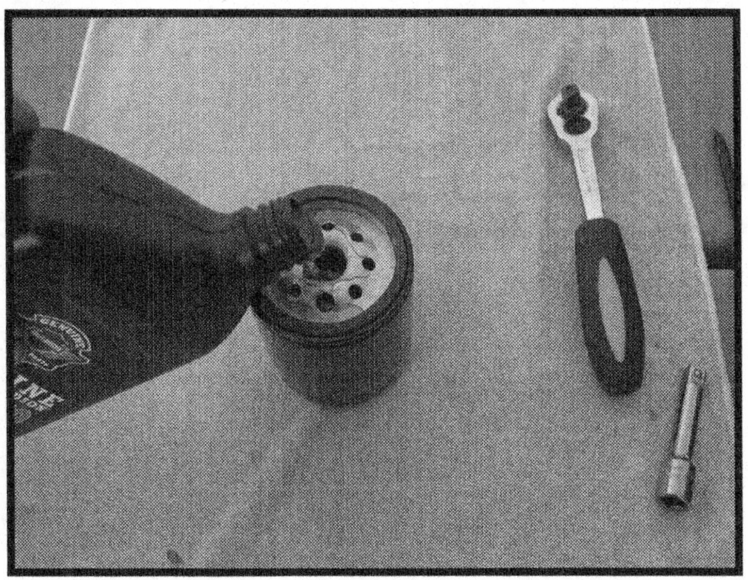

Fig. 22. Priming the Oil Filter With New Oil

Swirl the oil filter so the oil is absorbed by the filter media. See Fig. 23 and add more oil until the filter media cannot absorb any more oil, or is very close to saturation. The oil filter should now have about ½ full of oil sitting inside of it.

The method here is used to prevent the engine from running dry without oil for a few seconds when started up after changing the oil. Priming the oil filter needs to be performed, but some unskilled mechanics do not bother and that can cause you trouble down the road from excessive engine wear after each oil change! Whenever you have other repair shops change your morotcycle's oil ask the mechanic to prime the new oil filter with fresh oil, please.

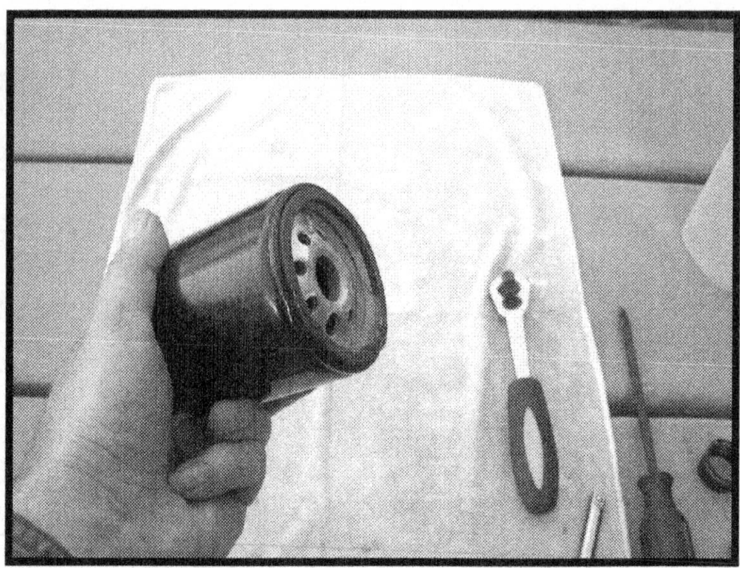

Fig. 23 Swirling the Oil to Prime the Oil Filter

Fig 23 shows the filter being tilted on the side and swirled, so the oil inside is absorbed by the internal pleated paper filter media.

This priming of the oil filter is very important as it prevents engine damage on start-up after draining the engine of its oil during routine oil changes.

Warning: If a untrained mechanic forgets to do this (some do) when the bike is started it runs dry of oil and you can hear the engine grinding itself to pieces for a few seconds. This has just taken three to five thousand miles off the life of your engine, or more.

If you know of people who have had earlier than normal engine failure it is likely caused by not priming the oil filter or not frequently changing the engine oil or using inferior oil in the engine. Most of the time engine damage will be traced back to failing to prime the oil filter with oil.

Fig. 24 Oiling the O-Ring

Dip your finger in the oil and wipe it along the top-side of the large rubber o-ring. It is okay to saturate the o-ring with oil, but only a little coating of oil is all that is really needed. See. Fig. 24.

Also, wipe some oil on the filter's pipe threads in the large center hole so the filter will not freeze up on the engine. Antisieze compound is not needed here, a dab of engine oil will work just fine.

OIL FILTER TIPS

Buying a new oil filter should not be troublesome as the stock Harley Davidson oil filter is a very high quality product and will perform all the filtering your engine needs. There is no need to spend a lot of money on aftermarket oil filters that claim to filter down to low microns. In fact, there have been motorcycle engines damaged by aftermarket oil filters that were not compatible to the engine's requirments and some can not be easily removed. The HD brand filter is just fine.

Fig. 25 Oil Filter with a Magnet Applied

This is the old engine oil filter on the bike that we are going to remove. It is the black canister shown in Fig. 25. Now is a good time to install the oil drain pan as shown under the bike's forward section of the engine.

I have a chrome plated magnet on this filter. It helps to trap very fine metal filings inside the oil filter so they will not get circulated with the oil. These small filings are very abrasive like sandpaper and will wear an engine down quickly in no time. You can buy the magnet at any hardware store. It just snaps into place and stays put and only costs a few dollars. Get one on your bike!

Note: your Harley Davidson Dealer may have better, stronger magnet than shown in Fig. 25. These magnets really do work to trap highly abrasive steel metal particles that otherwise will circulate in the oil wearing out your engine.

Fig. 26 Oil Filter Removal

In Fig. 26 you can see the oil filter wrench is applied, the wrench is turning counterclockwise to loosen and the oil is now draining out of the filter. Notice how dirty black that oil is. Actually, it is just a photographic lighting problem. The oil is actually clean in this bike due to using the perpetual oil change method described in this book. See Fig. 27.

Yes, it will make a mess as shown in Fig. 27. Yes, you can buy a plastic device that helps drain the oil away from the case, but most pros don't bother with it. Why? The bike needs to be cleaned anyway after oil changing so we will clean up the mess then at one time.

See the slot in the oil filter socket wrench in Fig. 26. It was used to install the oil filter socket past that knob on the right. It is the crankshaft position sensor and you need a slotted filter wrench to get the filter wrench past the sensor.

You can use a strap wrench, but they don't work so well in tight places like this. Just go buy a Twin Cam oil filter socket. You will need this special tool. Any Harley dealer can sell you one and they are not expensive.

Emergency - stuck filter problem: What if the oil filter wrench will not remove the filter because it is so tight and the filter socket strips away the filter casing? The special oil filter wrench will not remove a stuck oil filter as it will easily strip the filter's thin metal edges. You can try a strap wrench, but most of the time you are going to have to drive a long screwdriver handle clear through the filter, then crank it out. Before doing this contact an automotive parts store as they also sell adjustable filter wrenches that will grab even stripped heads on oil filters. But if they don't have one? Then brutality is required to destroy that stubborn oil filter!

I did not show the procedure, but it is easy to do. Just tap with a hammer a long thick sharp-ended screwdriver through the filter case, through the filter media and out the other side. Be careful not to pound so hard that the screwdriver goes past the filter case and penetrates your aluminum engine case! Be gentle here.

Now slide the oil drain pan under the filter area of the bike, pull the screwdriver handle down (counterclockwise) and the filter will break free. Yes, it is a messy job and appears primitive, but it works. Some aftermarket oil filters are more prone to get stuck on the engine, so use Harley Davidson brand oil filters.

Over-tightening the oil filter causes them to become stuck like this. You just want a snug fit for the oil filter. About ½ turn past the point where the rubber o-ring makes contact with the engine case.

HAND PROTECTION

Used oil can have harsh acids and chemicals that some people may find irritating. Regardless, it is always a good plan to apply a hand protectant salve to the skin or wear disposable rubber gloves so nothing can be absorbed into your body from skin contact with new or used oil.

Fig. 27 Yes, Dirty But Is Easily Cleaned

Here the oil filter is removed and oil has dripped everywhere and still draining. Make sure you have installed the oil drain pan to catch the used oil before removing the engine oil filter.

Note: make certain the old oil filter still has its rubber o-ring on the filter. Make sure no part of this old o-ring remains on the engine case. The engine case mating surfaces should appear polished and clean metal as seen in Fig. 27 and 28.

Notice how clean the oil is dripping from the shinning metal surfaces. When you use the perpetual oil change method in this book your engine oil will always be clean and will never get very dirty.

Dirty oil is abrasive like sandpaper. If you can keep oil clean it is going to make your bike run many more trouble-free miles than many other bikes will. Many thousands of miles is to be gained!

Fig. 28 Cleaning Oil Surface on Engine Case

Clean up the mating circular metallic surface as shown in Fig. 28 with a clean rag. This is where the oil filter's o-ring seal will meet. Fresh oil dripping on the surface is okay after you wipe the surface clean the first time. Oil will keep leaking from the center oil bolt as shown.

THE NAME MAY CHANGE

The name of the motor may change, but this book will not be outdated. Harley Davidson is reworking its Dyna engine and it may replace the Twin Cam 88 engine in the future, with a different name.

You will likely find no change in the oil change procedure. If there is a change it will likely be very minor. Visit our Website for any updates you may need to know about.

JamesRussellPublishing.com

Wipe up any excess oil from the engine case under the filter at this time. Don't clean it or apply any chemicals or soap, just wipe as shown to soak up excess oil. Make sure no grit or sand particles are on the circular metallic surface. It must be clean.

Note: Do not press hard when wiping up oil as there could be some sharp edges here on the engine case to cut your finger.

Now install the oil filter by hand. Turn the filter by hand all the way until the filter's o-ring stops against the sealing surface. Only then will we use a wrench to slightly snug the oil filter.

Note: most manuals will tell you never to use a wrench to tighten any oil filter. Yes, you can use your hand, but it is hard to do with so little clearance to fit your hand around the filter to tighten it. Also, with oil film on the filter and your hands it is all the more harder. We don't want leaks, so we will use the wrench to make it easier to rotate.

Fig. 29 Snug Tighten Only On Oil Filter

Just give the oil filter a ½ turn more clockwise turn just so the oil filter is snug. We don't need to have this thing tight. Just snug. We don't, however, want any leaks of oil as it will wet the rear tire of the motorcycle and could cause a crash. This is rare to happen, as most leaks will only be a small drip if it does leak, but we want no leaks here anyway.

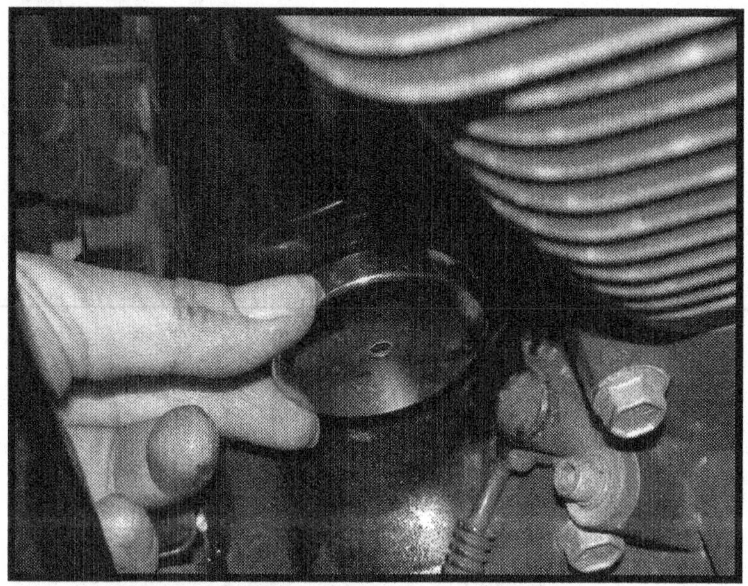

Fig. 30 Magnet Installed On The New Oil Filter

Reinstall the oil filter magnet as shown in Fig. 30.

ENGINE STARTING PROCEDURE

Now we can start the engine. Before we start the engine:

1. Install negative battery lead if you removed it.
2. Turn off the handlebar kill switch.
3. Remove oil pan from under the bike.
4. Remove all tools near, on or under the bike.
5. Remove any wood blocks from under the side stand.
6. Wipe up any oil spills on the ground.
7. Sit on the bike so it is level.
8. Turn on the ignition switch and start it up.
9. Let it idle. Do not open the throttle.

Listen to the motor and watch the oil sending light on the dashboard. That light should go out in less than two seconds. If not, shut off the engine right away.

If the engine oil pressure light did not shut off, check to make sure there is no gross leak from the oil filter. It will be a huge leak and you can't miss it. This could happen if somehow the oil filter o-ring fell off the filter or is folded or pinched. Rare, but it can happen. It can also happen if the old o-ring was not removed and now two o-rings are installed between the engine case and the oil filter.

Odds are, the oil pressure light will go out right away. Listen to the motor for any unusual sounds. If you primed the oil filter odds are you will hear no unusual noise. Let the bike's engine run for at least 30 seconds and then shut it off. Check the oil level in the oil tank.

The oil level should have dropped a bit. Add very little oil as the oil tank fills quickly, about ¼ of a quart on each try. Let's get the oil at least on the lower dipstick mark which should be about a ½ filled oil tank or close to it.

Note: To check the oil on the oil tank the dipstick is always inserted all the way down as far as it can go then it is lifted to take an oil level reading.

The bike needs to be level so sit on the bike in the normal riding position when checking the oil level.

IMPORTANT: But first we need to start the bike and let it run for a minute, then shut it off. We should have seen the oil level drop a bit. Now refill the oil tank to the ½ way filled condition (half way between the low and high oil marks on the dip stick).

Yes, the engine oil should be checked when hot, so go take it a very short ride and when the engine is hot check the oil level again. If you need more oil, add a little bit more and retest using the dipstick. ***Make sure there is absolutely no oil on your tires!***

Fast Method: There is a faster method I use, but you should only use it after you have changed the oil a few times to get the feel of your bike how it handles oil. I just fill the oil tank to an inch below the full mark on the dipstick and drive away. When the oil heats up and expands it just fills to the full mark where it is supposed to be.

Your bike may need to be 2" below the full mark when cold to then expand to the full mark on the dipstick. Experimentation will guide you.

Remember do not overfill the oil tank. It is better to have a tank ½ filled than to have a tank overfilled. This is because of the dry sump oil pumping arrangement prefers it so. I aim for an oil tank that is ¾ full when the oil is hot.

NITROGEN TIRES

Did you know that instead of using air many race drivers, truckers and car tire dealers are switching from air to nitrogen when inflating tires? Yes, you can do this on your motorcycle too. Nitrogen is more stable at temperatures and leaks less than oxygen, but its prime benefit is maintaining correct tire pressure which saves fuel and maintains precise handling.

OVERFILLING THE OIL TANK

It is easy to overfill the oil tank. Just use a battery water filler squeeze bulb as shown in Fig.31 to suction out the oil. Very easy to do and this bulb will be used for the perpetual oil change method we will explain in this book.

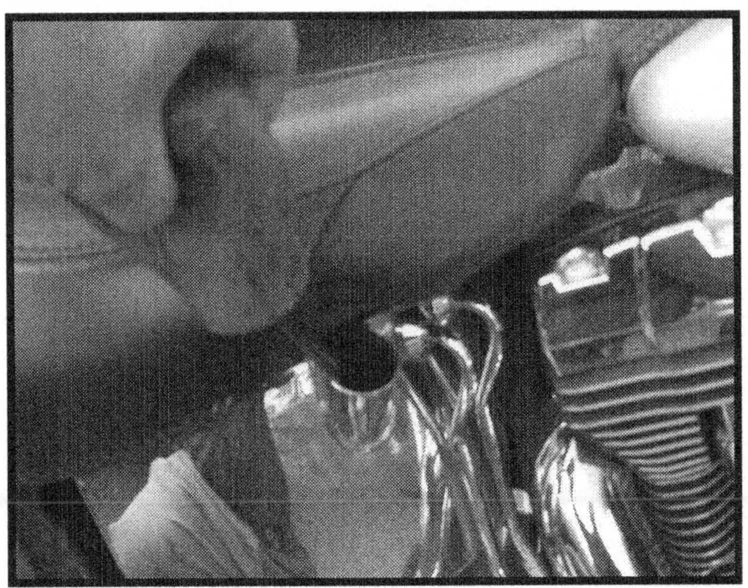

Fig. 31 Battery Squeeze Bulb Removes Oil From Oil Tank

Note: You can change the engine, primary case and transmission oil more often than the manufacturers' recommendations. With some high grade synthetic oils you can even go beyond general recommendations. However, if your bike is covered under a warrantee it is best to change the oil at the manufactures time and mileage intervals or sooner to preserve your warrantee.

Warning: Oil is slippery so make absolutely certain you wipe up oil spills right away so you or others will not slip or fall, but also if oil gets onto your motorcycle's tires you can crash as soon as you ride away. Always keep this in mind!

CHAPTER 4

PRIMARY CASE OIL CHANGE

Remember, you do not have to do this job today. You can do it tomorrow, even next week. It is easier to do each oil change on separate days for those who are new at doing this or if leisure time is restrictive.

I am experienced, and I still like to do each on separate days to appease my gift of laziness and to fulfill my heartfelt desire for a life of comfort and ease.

At least take a break between jobs so your mind will be better focused to the job at hand. There is never a need to rush. Just take your time and enjoy the procedure.

Here's the tools we will use to change the oil in the primary chain case. See Fig. 32.

1. Torx #40 socket.
2. Torx #25 socket.
3. 3/8" drive socket wrench.

That's all we need. But we will be using some Teflon paste (or ordinary plumber's pipe dope) for the oil drain plug threads. See Fig. 38.

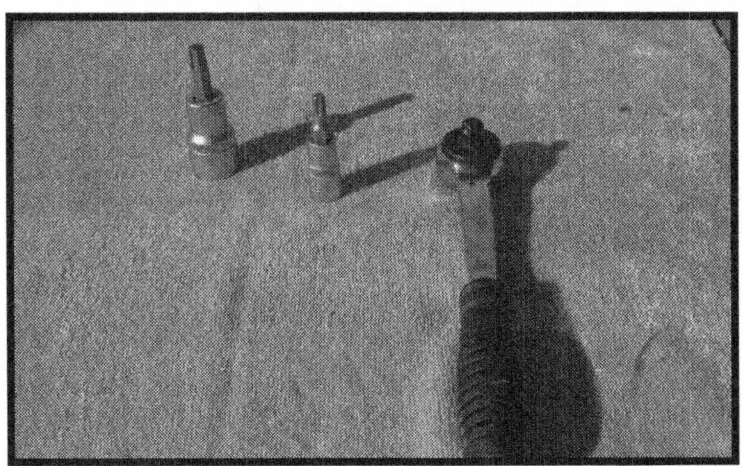

Fig. 32 Primary Case Tools

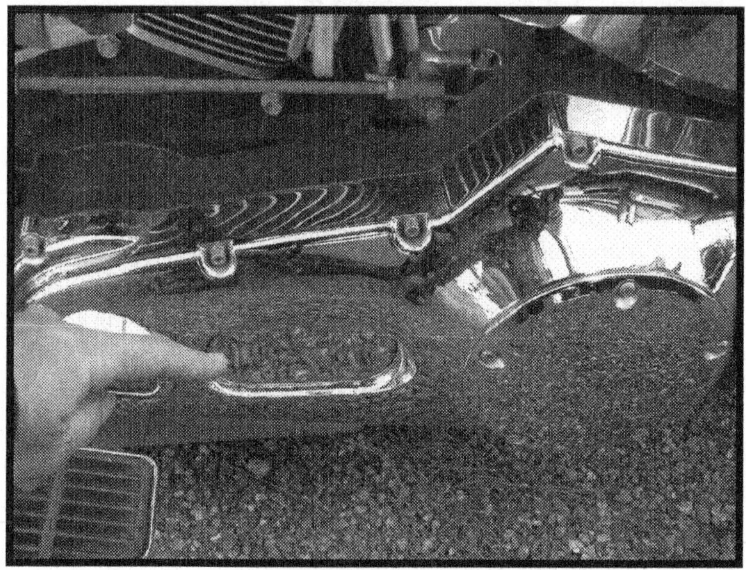

Fig. 33 Primary Chain Case Cover

In Fig. 33 I am pointing at the primary chain case cover, specifically at the oval inspection plate.

To the right is the large circular derby-cover (see Fig. 34). We will not even bother removing that derby cover, as we just want to remove the oval inspection plate. But first we need to find the oil drain.

DRY CLUTCH

There is really no reason to switch to a dry clutch unless you want the sound and look it gives on a custom bike and the fact you no longer need to change the primary case oil because there is no longer any case, just an exposed rubber primary drive belt.

The dry clutch can be troublesome. The factory wet clutch system is very reliable and troublefree. Just change the oil and all will be well.

Fig. 34 Locating Primary Case Oil Drain Plug

I want you to look at where my finger is pointed by the derby cover in Fig. 34. Note that it is just to the left of the screw at the 4 o'clock position. Now look under the primary case where I have pointed and you will see a small recessed Allen screw inserted vertically at the bottom of the case. That is the primary chain case oil drain screw. You can see it better in Fig. 35 and Fig. 36.

Let's remove this screw and drain the oil.

Fig. 35 Breaking Loose Primary Case Oil Drain Plug

We are just going to break free the oil drain plug so there is no oil pan under the bike, yet. We need some leverage and elbow-room to work as the bike is close to the ground. Use the larger Torx bit of the two for this job (T-40). See Fig. 35. Don't remove the oil drain plug, just break it free for now.

Note: if you must lift the bike a bit simply place a solid, flat wooden board under the kickstand. However, you really do not need to lift the bike.

Yes, those are Kingman, Arizona pine needles under the bike. That is where I wrote this book when I stayed there for the winter. I snowbird and travel a lot bringing my motorcycle with me everywhere I go.

This bike in the photographs is a 2002 Harley Davidson Fat Boy with 56,000 miles on it and it runs strong like it was brand new. I put over 22,000 miles a year on my bikes.

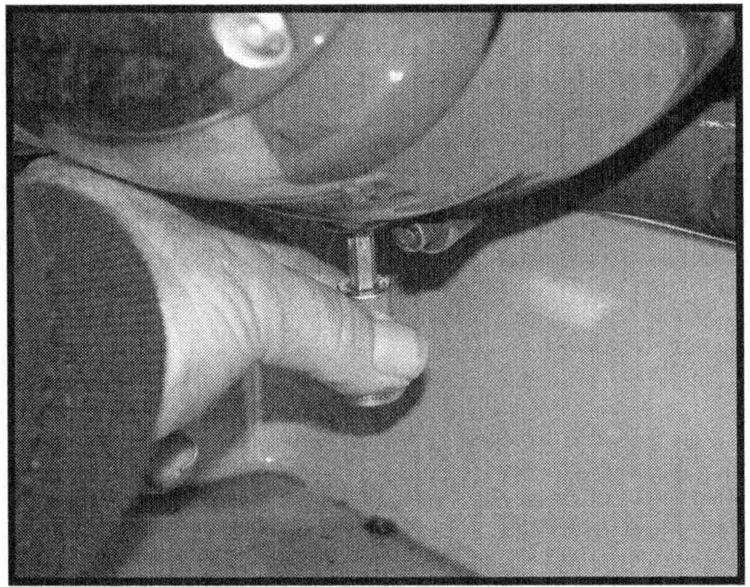

Fig. 36 Removing Primary Case Oil Drain Plug by Hand

Now is the time to get that oil pan under the primary case. If you do not want to buy an oil pan you can use a disposable aluminum baking pan, but using a dark color oil pan will help you see oil contamination; metal chips, etc.

Now remove the socket wrench and just unscrew the oil plug by hand using the Torx socket bit. We do this so that the oil plug will not cross-threaded itself or the case when using a powerful wrench to remove it. See Fig. 36 showing using fingers to remove the drain plug without the use of a wrench.

Note: cross-threading happens when the screw or bolt's threads initially do not match and a wrench is applied that forces the threads to mesh against each other. This cross-threading can also happen if a wrench is applied too soon on a loose screw or bolt, the force of the wrench (usually when cocked sideways a bit) can cause the threads on the screw or bolt to mesh adversely on each other and strip. This is why we insert screws, bolts and spark plugs in by hand pressure first as far as it will go, then we use the wrench to "gently" finish tightening the item. Only after the object firmly bottoms out is the final torque applied to tighten the item. But this primary case oil drain is different, it will never bottom out, so another procedure will be used to tighten the oil drain.

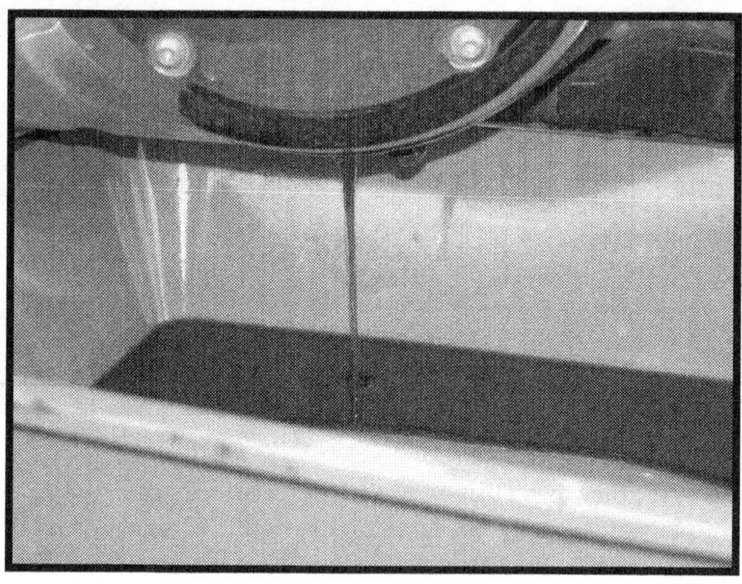

Fig. 37 Draining Primary Case Oil

In Fig. 37 we are draining the primary case oil. Yes, the oil is dirty black. This is because of the dark clutch material is wearing away which is normal so do not panic. You will also see small aluminum or steel dust in the oil. This too is normal as the chain and gears and clutch plates are metal and they do wear. There is no oil filter for the primary. If you saw this in engine oil it would be a cause for concern, but not here, this is normal.

As long as you see metallic dust all is well. If you see large pieces of metal then it is not normal and you will need to remove the primary cover and take a look inside. We are not going to do this in this book. Look for chips in the oil when you drain the used oil from the drain pan. The chips will stick to the bottom of the pan. A dark color pan is always best to use to easily identify the metal (or plastic) chips.

Just because you see a big metal chip does not mean you have a serious problem. It could have been an old chip from the initial break in period that has finally found its way out of the case with the oil. So do not panic if you see metal in the old primary oil you are changing. However, if you see a lot of chips in the oil of all different sizes then a problem exists and thankfully is usually easy to fix.

This is another good reason to do each job separately on a different day so that when you dump the oil and see metal chips you will not wonder which oil compartment they came from.

The best way to determine a problem with the primary system is to listen to it. If it is making noise it is likely the chain is slapping around a bit too loose. That will make a lot of metal chips appear in the oil. Adjust the primary chain, change the primary oil, problem solved.

If you change the oil in the same day, then make sure you inspect the oil drain pan for metal chips at each phase; once when changing engine oil, once when changing primary oil and once when changing transmission oil.

Fig. 38 Teflon Coated On The Primary Case Drain Plug

While we are waiting for the oil to drain completely we will clean the drain plug and apply Teflon paste (or plumbers pipe dope) to its threads. See Fig. 38. Let the oil drain as it is a slower process due to the small oil drain opening. Let's now remove the inspection plate cover using the small Torx socket (T-25).

Fig. 39 Using T-25 Torx Drive

Turn the Torx screw counterclockwise to loosen and remove the screws. See. Fig. 39.

You will now notice of the four screws, two are very short and two are very long. See Fig. 40.

Fig. 40 Inspection Plate Cover Screws

Fig. 40 reveals the primary case inspection plate and the screw arrangement without the gasket installed. Arrange the bolts as you see them here. The very shinny chrome is facing downward against the cloth rag. We are seeing the inside surface of the plate.

Let's now take a look inside the primary case inspection port.

Fig. 41 Primary Chain Tension Nut

If you look into the inspection plate hole this is what you will see in Fig. 41. That shinny nut is a 9/16" nut that holds the primary chain guide shoe. This shoe can barely be seen in the photo lifting the primary chain upwards. Raising the shoe tightens, down loosens. You can see the chain is forced upward by the shoe.

Normally, your primary chain will not need to be adjusted. If you place your finger inside the inspection plate you can feel the chain slack in the upper area. This part of the chain can't be seen in the photo. There should be about 5/8" movement of the chain. There is a large room for error here so do not panic if the chain is a bit looser (increased chain slack).

You are supposed to make this measurement by turning the chain to find the tightest spot. To do this you lift the bike's rear wheel off the ground, remove the engine spark plugs, put the bike in first gear and gently turn the rear wheel to move the primary chain.

We are not going to do this procedure. It is best that you have this service performed by experienced mechanics as things can go wrong that may require removing the entire primary outside cover or worse you can lose a finger or the bike could even fall over on you easily. But if you want to, you can do the job. Get a Harley Davidson Service Manual for your bike to learn the details involved to perform the job safely.

I will say that making the chain slack adjustment from inspection porthole is a bit inconvenient. You use a 9/16" socket with an extension to loosen the nut about two full turns and the shoe and chain will drop downward. You wiggle the wrench upward past the serrations on the backside of the plate to raise the chain back up again then tighten the nut. It is easy to do, but sometimes it takes a few tries to get it right.

The primary chain can feel loose with slack and still be okay. If it is not seriously hitting any metal inside the primary chain case it is normally just fine. It is not uncommon for a primary chain to run 30,0000 without needing an adjustment. Usually the chain needs to be adjusted after the 1,000 mile break in period then adjusted whenever as needed which normally is rarely adjusted.

So, at each oil change just check the primary chain tension to see if all is well. Normally, the chain will not need to be adjusted especially if you use Harley Davidson's SYN3 Synthetic oil, which we are going to use for this oil primary case oil change.

PRIMARY FACTS

The Harley Davidson primary drive system is close to perfection as the chain, sprockets, chain tention adjuster and clutch components are bullet-proof. You will likely never have any problems with this system as long as you own the bike!

Of course, drag racing, burnouts and other horseplay will take its toll. Usually oil leaks is the most problem you will find on the primary system, and most of them are easily resolved with installing a new gasket you can perform yourself.

Fig. 42 Inserting Primary Case Oil Drain Plug By Hand

Coat the primary case oil drain plug threads with Teflon pipe dope. You can put it on the threads thick so it will help seal oil seepage. Now insert the Torx oil drain screw by hand using your fingers as far as it will go to prevent any cross threading. See Fig. 38 and Fig. 42.

Now Stop and Read the Following

Warning: This Torx oil drain screw is actually a headless plug that meets with a machine thread (or slight taper pipe thread) in the chain case. Since the oil drain plug has no head it will "never" tighten up. You can actually keep on threading the thing right through the case!

Yes, it is an old design but all Twin Cam engines (all Harley Davidson primary cases in fact do this as of the year 2006 when this book was written).

So, we must use caution when tightening this oil plug with a socket wrench as it will never feel tight to you. A good rule of thumb is to tighten the plug until it is flush with the primary chain case and give it one more ½ turn. An older motorcycle will require you screw the plug in deeper due to thread wear.

If you have inserted the plug too deeply it can leak oil. Any oil leak here cannot be tolerated. So, back out the screw, dope it up again using the Teflon paste and reinsert it. If it still leaks you will need to go buy some Teflon tape and wrap the threads with it with two turns of tape then insert it. This usually always fixes the problem.

Fig. 43 Flush Fit And Just ½ Turn to Tighten Primary Oil Drain Plug

Fig. 43 - use very little wrench pressure to tighten this oil drain plug. It will never fully tighten up and you don't want to drive the plug too deep inside the case.

With experience, you will get a feel for when to stop turning this drain plug. Usually it is a feel along with visual reference to get it right. Just think "light snug fit" instead of "tight fit" and you will get it right every time. This screw will not loosen or vibrate out of place, so don't think you need to "sock this thing down" tight.

Harley Davidson one day may modify this drain plug to make it simpler to install by using drain plugs with o-rings and nut-heads on them like they do with the engine and transmission drain bolts.

What if you forget and drive that screw all the way? Well, if the screw is now inside the primary case that would require that you remove the entire primary cover to retrieve it. Hardly no one will drive it all the way into the case. The probable situation will be you drive it in too far and now the oil drain plug is loose and slowly weeps or seeps oil. Just wrap the threads with two or three wraps of Teflon tape and reinsert the plug into the case for a "light snug fit."

Worse case scenario: What if you accidentally strip the threads and the oil drain can't be retained? You can purchase a rubber plug repair kit at most auto parts stores. This will fix the problem fast and away you go. Later, you can buy a new case or have the damaged one drilled and tapped or have a thread repair Heli-coil inserted. The rubber plug repair method can be used on the oil drain on the Harley Davidson transmission if needed.

Never force anything that is supposed to be inserted easily by hand. Always use your finger-strength to insert oil drain plugs and spark plugs or any steel bolt being driven into soft aluminum.

Now that the primary case oil drain plug is installed let's add the oil.

Note: older Twin Cam engines with high miles on the odometer may need a higher viscosity (thicker) oil as a thinner oil will creep past old gaskets and seep oil. If this is your situation then do not use 100% pure synthetic oils in any of the engine compartments (engine, transmision, primary case). Just stay with the 20-50 weight standard Harley Davidson oil. Or, use a 50-50 blend of oil. You can even reduce the blend of oil to 90% standard oil and 10% synthethic oil. Why? Because the synthetic oil will treat the seals in the engine to last longer and give extra wear and tear protection.

CLUTCH LEVER EASE

The clutch on many Harley Davidson bikes built prior to 2006 had a hard pull on the clutch lever that can tire a rider's hand when in prolonged city traffic. If this bothers you Harley Davidson has a fix for this problem. It is best to have your Harley Davidson dealer perform this upgrade as it is a bit more involved for the novice to perform.

Fig. 44 Adding Synthetic Oil to Primary Case

We will add 1 quart of SYN3 synthetic oil to the primary case. You can even add 2 ounces of oil additive brand-named "Duralube" if you wish along with this 1 quart of oil. It will not overfill the case or harm the clutch.

I know the Harley Davidson service manual says to measure the oil from the clutch derby cover, but experience tells me that each time I do that I am still only adding 1 quart of oil. So, why bother removing the derby cover and have to keep replacing that huge 0-ring gasket which must be replaced each time? If you put one quart of oil into that primary case there will be plenty of oil in there and very close to a perfect measurement of oil if not spot-on target.

If you want to you can use the Harley Davidson Service Manual method to measure the oil level in the primary case, but the method can be slightly inaccurate if the bike is not perfectly level. I just add one quart of oil with 2 additional ounces of Duralube, seal it up and drive away. It works just fine.

Oil enhancement products (Duralube or other brand of liquid friction-reducing oil) may save you a ton of money on preventing excessive wear and tear if you believe what is printed on the product label as being true statements of fact. I have noticed that Duralube did quiet down the Harley Davidson valve train from noise, so it is doing something positive in the engine oil.

Note: if you plan on not using synthetic oil make sure you purchase Harley Davidson's primary case oil. It is different than engine and transmission oil. As of this writing, only the Harley Davidson's Syn 3 oil can be used in all three engine compartments. Harley Davidson, in the future, may have a new oil with a different name replacing Syn 3 with the same benefits. The Twin Cam primary case always requires one quart of oil, so always refill to one quart.

Note: Harley Davidson does not recommend using any oil additives as they believe it is unnecessary. We agree as long as you use a very high grade of oil in your engine such as using synthetic oil or synthetic oil blends. Some highly respectable motorcycle magazines rate many oil additives as "snake oil" and are useless. I believe the use of synthetic oil and blends are now so good that oil additives are not really needed anymore.

When you change the oil you will soon discover how much oil to add to your motorcycle. **Example**: Let's assume you drain your oil then pour the used oil back into the new oil containers and you have now discovered that you have drained out 3 quarts. Well, you simply need to pour in 3 quarts of new oil. The service manual may say pour in 3.5 quarts, but then you would be "overfilling" the engine with oil. Only a completely dry, internally cleaned engine (new engine or after an engine overhaul) would need that extra half quart of oil. So remember, what you remove, simply restore that same amount of oil.

The final measure is the dip stick and that will tell you what to add or subtract in the end. But using the method I just described will put the oil dead-on target each and every time. <u>But as you can see the primary case has no dip stick so you must add the same amount of oil you remove</u>.

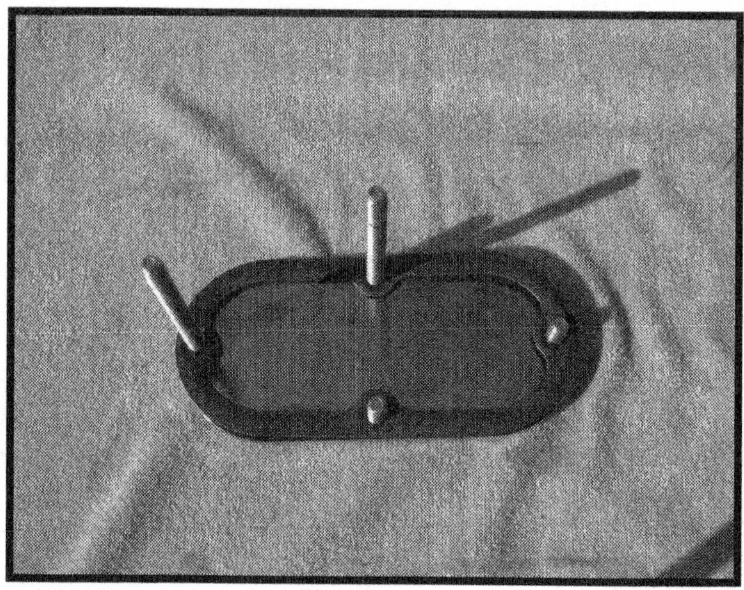

Fig. 45 Gasket is Installed

Note: If you prefer to remove the primary case derby cover you "must" replace the rubber o-ring as it deforms with heat and will not easily be reinstalled.

Here we have the inspection plate's gasket installed and ready to go. See Fig. 45. Believe it or not, you do not need to change this gasket each time you remove this inspection plate. There is no oil pressure inside the primary case to force oil out of the inspection plate.

The gasket does not seal against a pool of oil, but only sprayed oil so it only prevents seepage of oil. This means the gasket can be used many times, more than a half-dozen times before it will become hard, break and seep oil. Here I had to use a new gasket because after a year of using the old gasket it started to crack near the inner screw area (but it still sealed perfectly). You can put a new gasket on each time if you want, but many gaskets can be reused and this is one of them. Just put a new one on when you see it has become stiff. It is not critical.

When we replace the inspection plate we need to make sure the proper screws go into the proper holes.

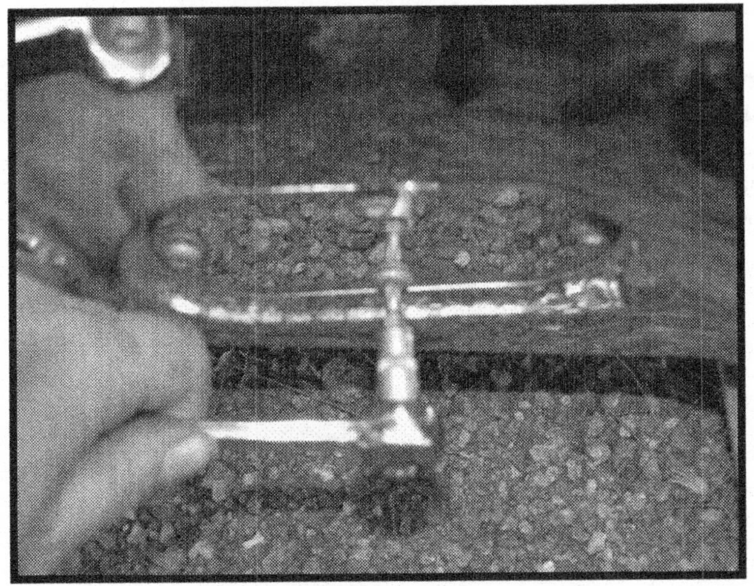

Fig. 46 Tightening the Torx Screws

In Fig. 46 you can see the cover in place. The plate's top long screw will go in the 12 o-clock position and the other long screw will be in the 3 o-clock position. The other two holes will be the small screws.

Now tighten the screws gently in a cross pattern. First tighten the top screw, then the bottom, then the left, then the right. Keep in that order giving a slight tightening to each.

When the screws are snug, give them all one more slightly more than snug tightening. Be careful not to over-tighten as the Torx head screws are prone to strip. These screws must be tightly snug or the oil will seep from the gasket, even from a brand new gasket.

Remember, if the inspection cover gasket leaks it will not drip oil. It will only seep oil that will make the gasket area appear dirty. You will not break down or lose your primary oil if this gasket is not sealed up perfectly. If you later see a seep, just snug it back up tight. Nothing to worry about.

Let’s change the transmission oil.

CHAPTER 5

TRANSMISSION OIL CHANGE

Fig. 47 Tools & Supplies for Transmission Oil Change

Note: if you plan on not using synthetic oil make sure you purchase Harley Davidson's transmission oil. It is different than engine or primary oil.

Here are the items we need for the transmission oil change.

1. Teflon paste thread sealant (pipe dope).
2. Oil drain plug o-ring.
3. ¼" Allen wrench.
4. 5/8" socket.
5. 3/8" socket Allen wrench.
6. 3" socket extension.
7. 3/8" drive socket wrench.
8. One quart of Synthetic SYN 3 or H.D. transmission oil (only 3/4 quart will be used).

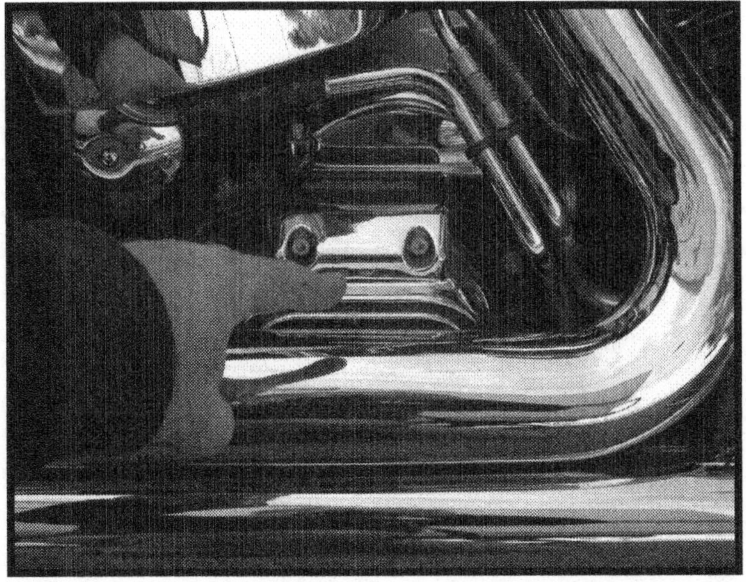

Fig. 48 Transmission Location Revealed

My finger is pointed at the location of the Twin Cam engine's transmission on the right hand side of the bike. See Fig. 48. On the right hand side of the transmission case you will see the oil dipstick location. In this engine it is chrome plated and flush with the case with an Allen head bolt that is the head of the transmission oil dip stick. See Fig. 55.

NO MYSTERY

Changing the transmission on all Harley Davidsons is no mystery. It is easy to do. Just find and remove the drain plug, locate the oil fill dip stick, replace the drain plug, add oil, replace dip stick and the job is done.

You can use this book's instructions to change the transmission oil on any V-Twin Harley Davidson motorycle. The Dyna, V-Rod and the Sportster will have a different procedure, but minor in detail.

Fig. 49 Removing Transmission Oil Drain Plug

To get to the transmission oil drain plug is a bit of a trick to do. It is well hidden from easy view. See Fig. 49.

Look under the bike and you will see what appears as two tin cans. These are the soft tail shock absorbers. Notice the wrench is being placed between them about an inch from the end (the end closest to the engine).

Sometimes, with a flashlight, looking along the frame and along the top of the shocks you may see the oil drain nut, but it is often so dirty it can't be seen, or accessories are in the way preventing a peek to see it.

Just fumble around by feel to get the socket onto the oil drain plug. As shown in Fig. 50, do not keep the socket on the wrench as in Fig. 49 if you have trouble getting the socket on the oil drain nut. Just use the 3" extension on the socket and try to find it by hand, first. This makes the procedure easy.

Fig. 50 Locating Oil Drain Plug by Hand Using Extension & Socket

Once you have the socket on the oil drain plug, then you can put the ratchet wrench on as shown in Fig. 49 and turn counterclockwise to loosen the oil drain bolt. It will likely be tight so don't let the socket slip off.

Caution: be ready for the drain plug to suddenly break free so you don't skin your knuckles.

Push the socket upward as you apply turning pressure to the wrench. We don't want the head of the oil drain plug to round-off.

Okay, remove oil drain plug and drain the oil (no photo is shown).

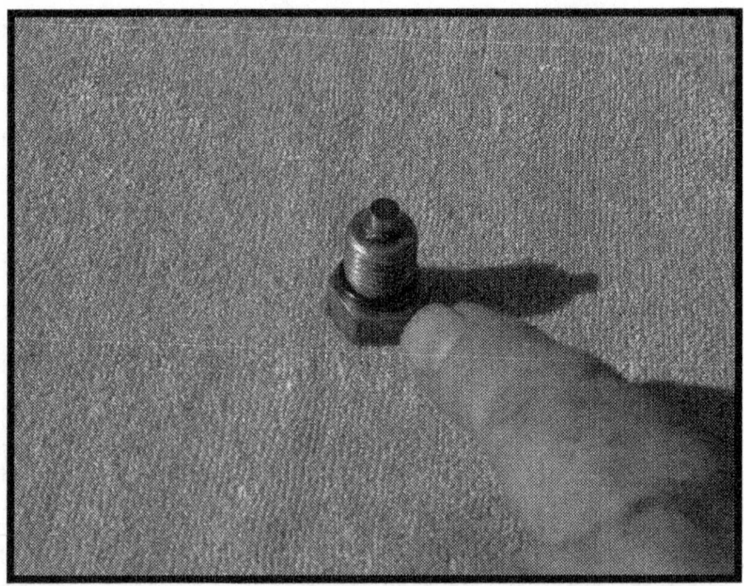

Fig. 51 Transmission Oil Drain Plug

The transmission oil drain bolt is identical to the engine oil drain bolt. You can even interchange them if need be. Here I have cleaned the bolt of metal chip dust and installed a new o-ring.

It is rare to find metal chips on the magnetic tip of the transmission oil drain plug, but sometimes there will be a fine haze from normal gear and fork wear. If you see a lot of metal, you need to start using the clutch better or stop horsing around speed-shifting as it is wearing out your transmission parts.

Tip: Never stomp on the shifter to shift gears. Use gentle shifting force. Stomping bends the internal shift forks then the gear dogs don't mesh correctly and the transmission fails prematurely. Wearing big heavy boots means you need to be aware of the strong force you are applying to the shifter. Ease up a bit.

Don't' panic if you see metal filings on the oil drain plug. It is when you see a lot of chips in the oil pan after draining the oil, only then it is high time to take corrective action to prevent further damage.

Put a new rubber o-ring on the drain plug then coat the threads with Teflon pipe dope as shown in Fig. 51 and in Fig. 52.

Now we will install the oil drain plug, but there is a problem:

Note: The problem is if you try to install the oil drain plug the same way you took it off using a socket it will not happen easily. The socket gets in the way as the bolt sits low inside the socket and the threads of the bolt will not meet the threads of the transmission. You end up spinning the wrench never to make a connection. Here's what we will do to stop this.

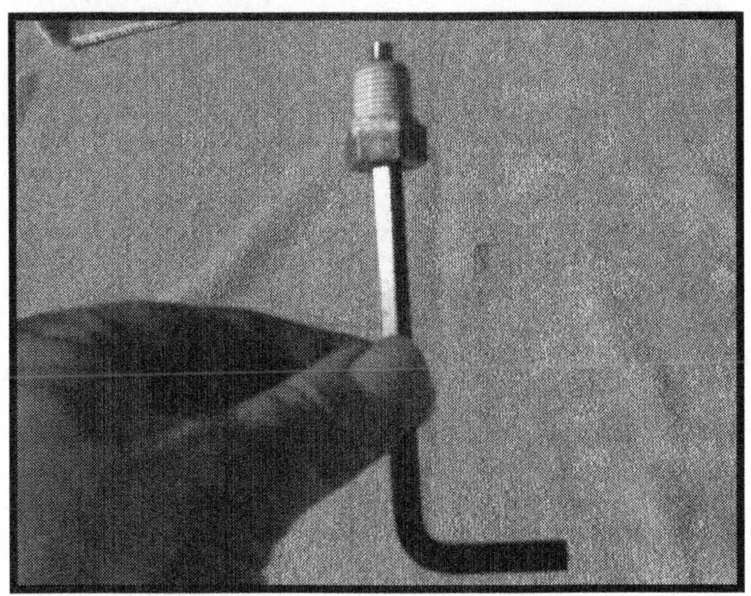

Fig. 52 Allan Wrench Inserted Into Drain Plug

Look closely at Fig. 52 as this is the assembly we are going to use to reinstall the transmission oil drain plug not using a socket wrench.

The oil drain plug has a new o-ring and the threads are painted with Teflon paste pipe dope. Notice the magnetic tip and the nut portion of the bolt is not coated!

Insert the long-end of the ¼" Allan wrench into the Allen hole as shown.

Fig. 53 Inserting Transmission Oil Drain Plug With Allan Wrench

Now look at Fig. 53 to see how we are going to install the transmission oil drain plug by hand into the transmission. Just slide the oil drain bolt up into the transmission and turn the Allen wrench clockwise. It is still a bit tricky to locate the threads, but it will get installed with a bit of practice. If you have a hard time, remember that this is your first time and the first time is always the most troubling for even us mechanics! It is hard to find the hole and line up the threads, but you will make the connection after a few tries. Be patient and keep trying! Using the Allan wrench in the drain plug as shown in Fig. 53 will make the job much easier to do.

Thread the oil drain bolt all the way, as far as it can go with the Allan wrench. This procedure makes certain we will not cross thread the threads. It would spell disaster to do so! Now let's go to Fig. 54.

Only then will we now apply the socket and ratchet to do the final tightening. Again, this is an o-ring bolt so it is going to feel like it is getting tight, but it may not be installed all the way in if you let up too soon. Let it get tighter and tighter as you screw it in.

Keep applying pressure to the wrench until the plug simply can't go anymore. It will stop hard like hitting a rock, just like it did when tightening the engine oil drain bolt. From this point you don't have to over-tighten the nut. Just snug is fine, once it stops hard against the transmission case. You will feel it when it happens.

Make sure this sudden stop occurs, as we do not want transmission oil dripping from a loose and improperly installed oil drain plug. It will drip to the back tire and could cause a slippery crash.

Fig. 54 Snug Tighten Only Transmission Oil Drain Plug

Fig. 55 shows the 3/8" Allen socket removing the oil fill dipstick on the upper transmission case. Turn counterclockwise to loosen and remove the dipstick.

Note: performing your first oil change is always a bit more difficult because you are unfamilair with everything involved. This is the learning process we all have to go through. The second time is real easy to do, now that you know how to do it!

Fig. 55 Loosening Transmission Dip Stick

The dipstick in Fig. 56 has an o-ring but you will hardly ever need to replace it, unless you have destroyed it somehow or it has baked and has become brittle with one year of age.

What should you do if you find it broken when touring? Just wrap the treads with Teflon tape (not paste) a couple times and then go to your dealer and get a new o-ring when you feel like it.

Keep in mind: the gaskets on an engine can last an incredibly long time, many years in fact. It is always standard procedure to not reuse gaskets and o-rings once they have been crushed by bolt pressure or cooked by heat (installed and fitted) but there are exceptions to this rule when there are zero pressures acting on the gasket such as the oil dip stick on the engine and transmission and the inspection plate on the primary chain case cover. In these instances you do not need to install new gaskets on the covers or install new o-rings on the dip sticks. Do not confuse this with the oil drain plugs. The o-rings on these plugs must always be replaced with new o-rings whenever the plug is removed.

What would happen if you forgot to install the rubber o-ring on the Twin Cam engine drain plugs? It would not produce a giant gushing oil leak and it will not drip oil too heavily, it would just seep oil slowly. In fact, by applying the Teflon pipe dope on the threads will actually seal the plug from leaks without the o-ring installed, but always do use a new o-ring anyway for a nice snug fit.

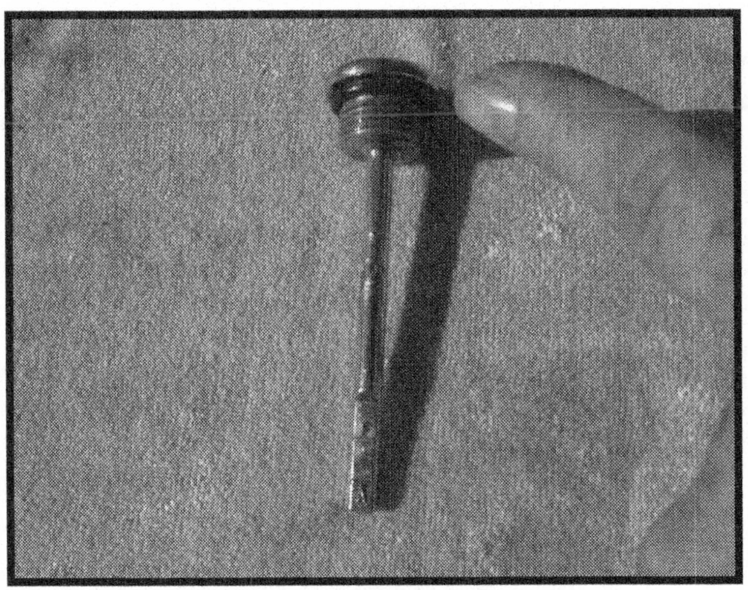

Fig. 56 Transmission Dip Stick

This dipstick has the upper mark “F” for full and the lower mark “A” for add oil. When we add new oil we want the mark at the “F” mark or just a bit under the line.

If you overfill it by accident and the oil rises a bit above the “F” line do not worry about it. If the oil level is touching the round portion of the shaft then suction out some oil using a squeeze bulb (See Fig. 31 to see a battery squeeze bulb).

UPGRADING TIRES

Have you tried upgrading your tires? When replacing tires look in a tire catalog and compare tires rated for highway use for cruiser motorcycles. You will get about 12,000 miles or more out of a good tire.

Make sure you examine the specifications and order the correct tire compound. A soft street compound, like steet sportbikes use, will wear fast and need replacing at around 6,000 miles. Not a good idea for a cruiser motorcycle.

Dunlop company (made in England) is making some nice smooth-riding, long-lasting formulas for the cruiser market. Metzeler also makes some nice tires (made in Germany). I have seen 15,000 miles on these tires used on my heavy cruiser bikes. Avon is another quality tire manufacturer I have used with great success (made in England).

Try upgrading your tires to the best money can buy and you will see a smoother ride, better balance, handling, braking and safety.

Let us not forget that the rubber tires is all that separates you from the harsh roadway. Invest in the best!

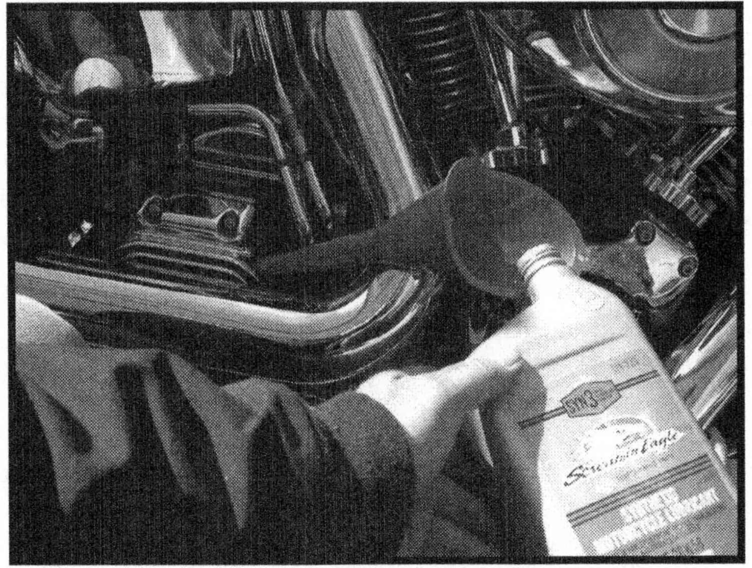

Fig. 57 Adding Synthetic Oil to Transmission

The bike does not need to be level. Just keep it on its side stand for now.

Using a funnel in Fig. 57 we will be adding Harley Davidson SYN3 Synthetic oil to the transmission. This synthetic oil is best to be used as it conditions the seals to avoid seal failure and will increase the horsepower and fuel mileage of the bike by reducing gear oil friction drag. Also, it is just going to make your transmission last a very long time.

We will only be adding about ¾ of a quart, so go slow and check the oil a few times.

After adding some oil, sit on the bike so it is level or at least close to being level and wait three seconds for the thick oil to equalize. It is like molasses. Now reach down and insert the dipstick into the hole all the way to the threads, but do not screw in the dipstick. The bike does not need to be perfectly level, just sit on the bike in a normal riding position.

Note: If you can't reach the dipstick when sitting on the bike place the transmission in first gear then you can place some flat planks of wide, thick wood under the side kickstand so the bike is close to level. Be careful as the bike could now fall over on to its right side. Tie a rope from the left handlebar to a very solid object to stop this toppling over from happening. Now you have a level bike and you can dip the dipstick without sitting on the bike. Or simply ask someone to sit on the bike for you if anyone is available. Better yet...

Helpful Advice: I believe you will find it easier to measure the oil you removed and just add that amount back into the transmission. I have found it only requires 3/4 quart of oil and it measures just right on the dip stick. No fuss, no mess, no delays, no hassles and it works!

Try not to let the dipstick touch other metal components as you dip the stick as a drop of oil can be planted on it and give you a very false reading. Keep dipping the stick a few times until you get the hang of it and you get consistent oil level readings.

Fig. 58 Checking Oil Level on Transmission

Transmission Oil Change

In Fig. 58 the dipstick is being dipped into the transmission while the bike is in the normal level riding position. Keep dipping a few times until oil level readings are consistent.

Generally, if you remove ¾ quart of old oil all you have to do is add ¾ quart of new oil and drive away. Just like what we did in the Primary Chain Case.

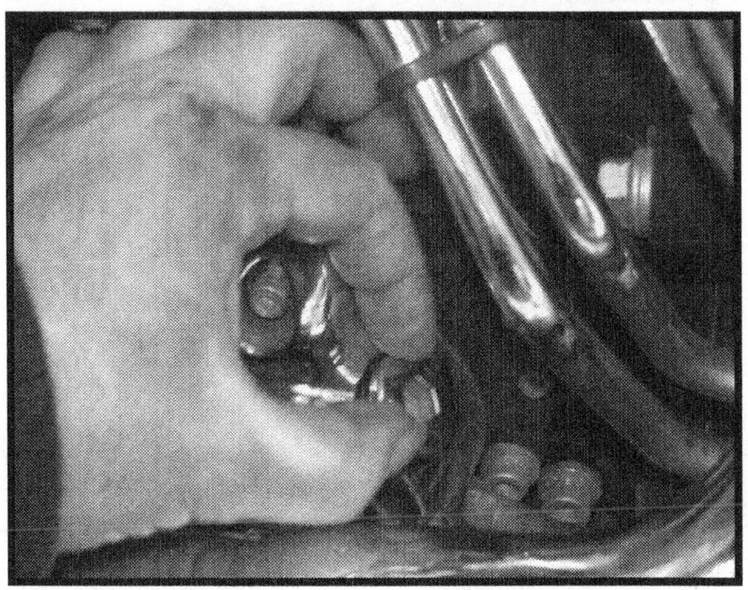

Fig. 59 Replacing the Oil Dip Stick in Transmission

We are now inserting the dipstick to tighten with our fingers only. Tighten all the way it can go then we will use the 3/8" Allen socket to snug it down. It need not be overly tight, just snug. There is no oil pressure in the transmission. The o-ring here will hold the dipstick in place quite well on its own.

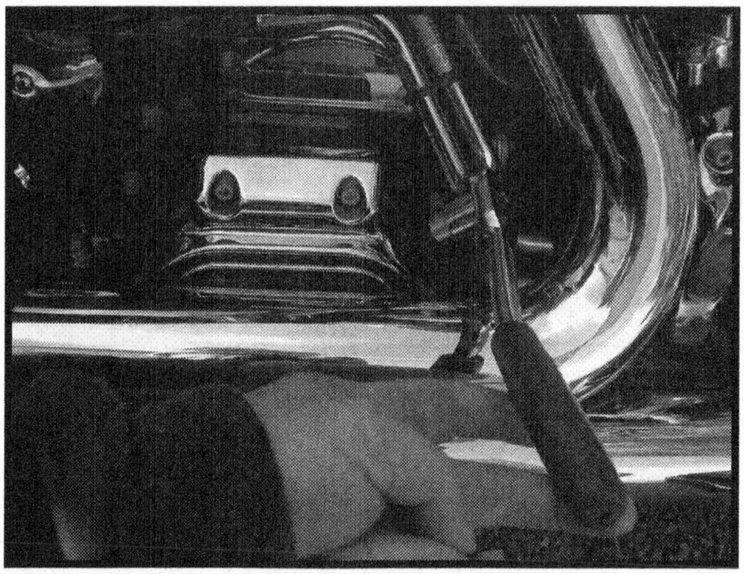

Fig. 60 Light Tightening of the Dip Stick

Fig. 60 reveals the two-finger method of tightening sensitive nuts and bolts that you do not want to strip. By using two fingers you can't apply huge globs of pressure to strip things. Use this technique when tightening spark plugs too.

We have finished changing the oil in the transmission. Let's now go change the engine spark plugs.

Warning: before starting up the motorcycle or driving away place the bike's transmission in neutral and remove any tools or wood blocks from under the bike and any wood planks under the side stand if you have used any of these items. Make sure your tires do not roll into any oil spills. Check your tires and make sure no oil is on them from any accidental oil spills before starting up the motorcycle. Keep your workplace clean at all times and wipe up any oil spills right away. Being sloppy will one day create trouble. Be neat and orderly at all times and you will reduce accidents to zero.

CHAPTER 6

CHANGING THE SPARK PLUGS

Fig. 61 Tools & Supplies to Change Spark Plugs

Here are the items we need to change spark plugs in the Twin Cam engine.

1. Feeler gage with a spark plug gap tool attached.
2. Aluminum base anti-seize compound.
3. Spark plugs (we use Accel U-groove Platinum plug Y2418P in this book).
4. 18 millimeter spark plug socket (for the Accel plug style) or
5. 5/8" spark plug wrench for Harley Davidson Screaming Eagle plugs.
6. 3/8" drive ratchet.

You only need one or the other of items 4 or 5. It depends on what type of spark plug you want to use. We use the high performance Accel-brand plug that needs a metric spark plug socket. This plug can give a two horsepower increase to your motorcycle and the fuel burns nice and clean increasing fuel mileage. It is not a hot or cold plug so it is safe to use in a stock or a stage-one tuned engine.

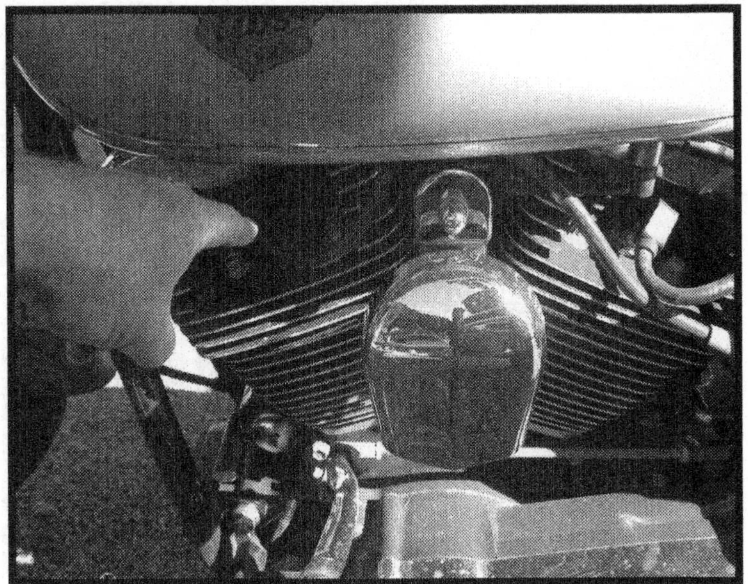

Fig. 62 Location of Front Cylinder Spark Plug

The location of the spark plugs are shown on the left side of the bike's engine in Fig. 62 and 63.

SPARKS FLY

When you purchase spark plugs make sure you get the right heat range. Spark plugs come in different heat ranges and installing the wrong plug can actually burn a hole in the piston! When in doubt, just buy original Harley Davidson spark plugs designed for your engine.

Fig. 63 Location of Back Cylinder Spark Plug

You remove the spark plug wires by simply pulling them away, but make sure you are holding on to the thick rubber boot section that is on the spark plug itself (see Fig. 63) when doing so. Pulling the wire may cause the wire to separate from the boot. Fig. 67 shows you the proper way to hold the boot when removing the wire.

POOR CONNECTIONS

Amazingly bikers break down for the simple things such as a burned fuse or a corroded spark plug wire terminal. Shine a flashlight into the rubber boots of the spark plug wires. You should see shinny metal. Any rust or green color on the electrode wire terminal is corrossion.

Also check the wire connectors to the ignition coil. You can see them in Fig. 63 behind a chrome cover. Check for loose connections. They all should be snuggly fitted.

Fig. 64 Gaping the Spark Plug

We gap both spark plugs to .038 of an inch using a feeler gage. Fig. 64 shows the spark plug gap adjustment tool being used to widen the gap. The gap we are speaking of is the curved ground portion residing over the spark plug's center electrode. We adjust the ground electrode's space above the electrode to measure .038 of an inch.

If your feeler gauge does not have a single gage strip that measures .038 you can use two strips that will equal the total. Example: use a .030 and a .008 to equal .038. We have done this in Fig. 64.

FUSES

Do you know where "all" of your fuses are located on your motorcycle? Do you carry spare fuses with you in your saddlebags all of the time? If not, you should. What are you going to to if a fuse burns out on a lonely back-streach of road in the middle of the night and you have no headlight or the engine fails?

Fig. 65 Checking the Gap With Feeler Gage

Here in Fig. 65 we are checking the gap. The feeler gage slides in and out with a slight friction drag.

Important: Set the spark plug gap as recommended by Harley Davidson's service manual when using Harley Davidson brand spark plugs. We are using a different brand of spark plugs in this book.

SPARE PLUG

In your toolbag you should have a spare set of spark plugs and a spark plug socket and wrench. A bad batch of gasoline can foul the plugs and leave you stranded. It happens!

A new set of plugs, even with bad gas, will often work just fine until you can refil your gas tank once again on the next fill up.

Fig. 66 Light Tap Closes Gap

If the gap is too wide then hold the spark plug vertically and then very gently tap the ground electrode against a hard surface to close the gap. If it is now too tight, just use the gap tool to bend the ground wire to widen the gap.

You may be wondering why you can't use the spark plug gap tool to close the gap. It is because they do a good job of opening the gap, but often do a poor job of closing the gap. They have a habit of twisting the ground wire out of shape. By tapping the ground wire against a hard surface the ground wire and the electrode will remain in perfect alignment with each other.

CELL PHONE

Carry a cellular telephone with you when you travel. Have one in your saddlebag with two batteries nearby, but uninstalled, so they will stay charged longer and can not be accidently turned on and the battery is run down to zero charge. A cell phone with a dead battery is useless.

Fig. 67 Holding Spark Plug Wire Boot

Go ahead and remove the spark plug boots from both cylinders. Remember to pull the wires by the thick rubber boot as shown in Fig. 67 and 68.

These “Thunderbolt” brand of spark plug wires are aftermarket high-performance wires and will give from two to as much as five horsepower increase. They will last the life of the bike. There are other brands of spark plugs and wires that can perform equally well.

Your Harley Davidson dealer may sell a set of high performance wires.

WIRES

Should you upgrade to high performance spark plug wires on a stock bike? No, it is not a requirement, but often you can get more power and fuel milage by using a higher quality spark plug and a wire set combined. You may gain two horsepower more in many cases, but you need to realize you will not be able to feel that small horsepower increase. You can feel an increase of five horses. You may see better fuel milage.

Fig. 68 Clean Area Around Spark Plug Before Removing

After removing the spark plug wires look to see if there are any grains of sand residing below the nut of the spark plug. When you remove the plug you don't ever want dirt or sand to fall into the cylinder. It will ruin your engine the moment you start it up.

Now is a good time to hose this area with some soap and water and wipe dry with a clean rag. Do this on both cylinders. Now we are ready to remove the spark plugs.

HOW OFTEN?

Change the spark plugs each 10,000 miles. Inspect them each 5,000 miles when you perform your oil change. If the plugs appear black but are still sparking (not fouled) consult your dealer on how to fix the problem. It may be just a rich fuel mixture, a lean condition or oil migration into the cylinder and the latter condition would require an engine top-end overhaul or use a hotter heat range spark plug to burn off the oil.

Fig. 69 Place Socket on the Spark Plug Then Tighten by Hand, First

Here I have place the spark plug socket onto the spark plug by hand to make certain it fits snugly. Some sockets have a sponge inside to protect the ceramic insulator. If so, you need to push the socket downward and twist it back and forth to make sure it penetrates the sponge and is actually gripping the spark plug nut firmly.

When you are sure the socket is installed snugly and firmly and you have twisted the socket down as far as it will go by hand (Fig. 69) only then can you insert the wrench to the socket (Fig 70).

Fig. 70 Wrench on Socket to Break Free a Spark Plug

We had to make certain the socket is deeply inserted and firmly gripping the spark plug nut as shown in Fig. 70. Why? Because the cylinder head is made of aluminum and the spark plug threads are made of steel.

Steel will cut aluminum with ease. We do not want any cross-threading here. It can happen just by turning the spark plug with a wrench and the wrench being sideways, tending to unscrew (or screw in) the spark plug, in a cock-sided wobble.

Notice how square the wrench is to the socket. You should place your other hand on the wrench near the socket whenever you loosen or tighten the spark plug to make sure no side forces are acting on the spark plug. Fig. 70 shows that if I put a lot of force on the wrench it will tend to bend the spark plug toward me and that can cause a spark plug's threads to start cutting and jump into the aluminum threads stripping them.

You will understand this more as you do this a few times with experience under your belt. Or just ask a mechanic about how to remove and install plugs without stripping the threads for more advice. I will show you more tips, so please continue reading.

Okay, break free the spark plug by applying a counterclockwise turn to the wrench.

Fig. 71 Unscrew Spark Plug By Hand

We only use a wrench to break free the tight spark plug. We never use the wrench to unscrew the spark plug when we can do it by hand. This way we will not strip the threads. See Fig. 71. We are removing the plug by hand turning counterclockwise using the socket on the spark plug as a hand grip.

Most all stripping of the threads is caused by using a wrench to unscrew (or screw-in) spark plugs. The plug's threads are actually quite loose in the cylinder and the plug will easily wobble around if its base is not in full contact with the cylinder head. So, by using your hand to install and remove the spark plugs as far as you can you can remove the spark plug without risk of stripping threads.

Note: stripping spark plug threads in aluminum cylinder heads is to be avoided at all costs. Repairs are expensive. Follow the instructions in this book and you should have no troubles.

Helpful Tip: you can place a sheet of rubber around the spark plug socket and that will give your fingers a stronger and better grip to turn the plug. It works better than using your slippery oily fingers. It's the same rubber used to open bottle and jar lids. This rubber will let you remove a snug plug without using a wrench in many cases. Some mechanics use a rubber length of hose to fit over the socket or spark plug and then turn the rubber hose to remove the spark plug.

On some bikes you just have to use a wrench as the threads are just tightly fitted. If so, you must go slow and easy and make sure the spark plug is not being subjected by any sideways forces by the wrench. Hold the socket end with your other hand as you turn the wrench to keep the pressure from bending the socket in any lateral direction. We only want a turning force to be applied to the spark plug.

Notice in Fig. 70 I am gripping the wrench handle with a very loose grip. It is not a tight-fisted grip. This way easy pressure is always applied to the spark plugs.

WHAT KIND OF SOCKET?

Sockets come in standard, short, long and thin-wall. With most motorcycles, purchase a spark plug socket to fit a 3/8" drive and select the short, thin-wall type. It will do the job very well.

When buying other standard sockets for working on your Harley Davidson make sure you purchase the 12-point socket as the standard 6-point size will not work. In Fig 70 you can see the cylinder head bolt is a 12-point, it has a star shape. However, the 12-point socket will still work with the standard square shaped bolt heads too. Buy the 12-point sockets!

Fig. 72 Washers & Electrode Tips on the Spark Plugs

These are the two old sparkplugs that were removed in Fig. 72. I want to point out to you those crush washers. One on each spark plug. Make sure they are still on the spark plug when you remove them. If not, you will find one still stuck to the base of the cylinder head. You have to remove it with a tiny knife blade or screwdriver.

Why? Because the extra gasket will prevent the sparkplug to sit inside the cylinder deeply and this will fail to ignite and completely burn the fuel. The cylinder will run rich and will actually be like retarding the engine timing. This will ruin engine performance and fuel mileage and will increase wear and tear on the cylinder with increased carbon buildup on the piston rings and valves.

BRAKE PADS

Someday you may want to learn how to change your own brake pads and perform other repairs. Again, if you look, you will notice you will need that 12-point socket to do the job.

At the left side of the spark plug do you see the golden (or silver) tips? They too must be present or it is stuck inside the rubber boot of the spark plug wire, or stuck inside the foam rubber within the spark plug socket tool. Some engines don't use these tips, but use bare threads to make the electrical connection. The tips shown in Fig. 72 are removable by using pliers to unscrew them from the spark plug. You won't have to do this with a stock Harley Davidson Twin Cam motor.

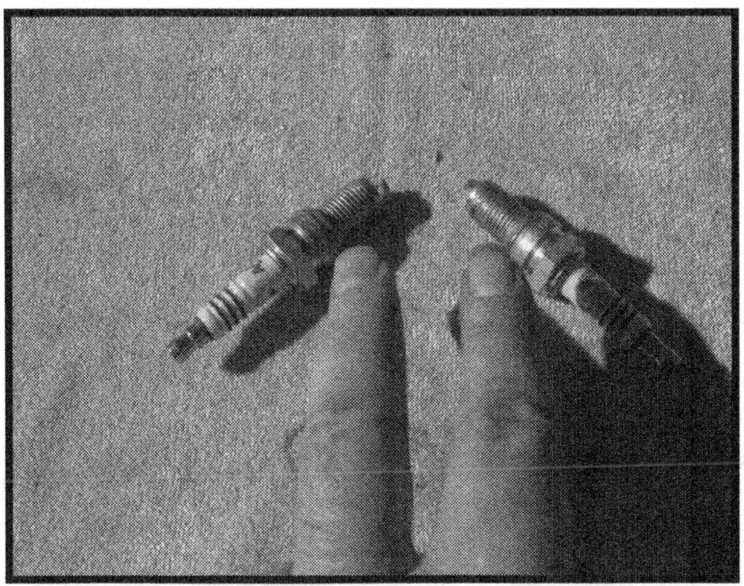

Fig. 73 Gaskets Snug to Plug's Base with Anti-seize Lubricant On Threads

Here in Fig. 73 we are blessing the spark plugs! Every good mechanic will do this. Actually my fingers are pointing at those washers on our brand new spark plugs. Screw them along the threads so they rest snugly as shown against the plug's base.

Now coat the threads with aluminum base anti-seize compound. Why? It acts as a lubricant to make installation easier. It keeps the plug threads from welding together that makes removal of the spark plugs difficult (or impossible in some cases). Don't worry, it is electrically conductive and will permit the plugs to spark as designed.

Note: I do not show it, but the gold (or silver) electrode tips on the plugs are often loose. Get some pliers and give them a mild but snug tightening so they will not become loose. A tight connection here will make for stronger and more reliable sparks and keep corrosion away from humidity, rain water and bike washings.

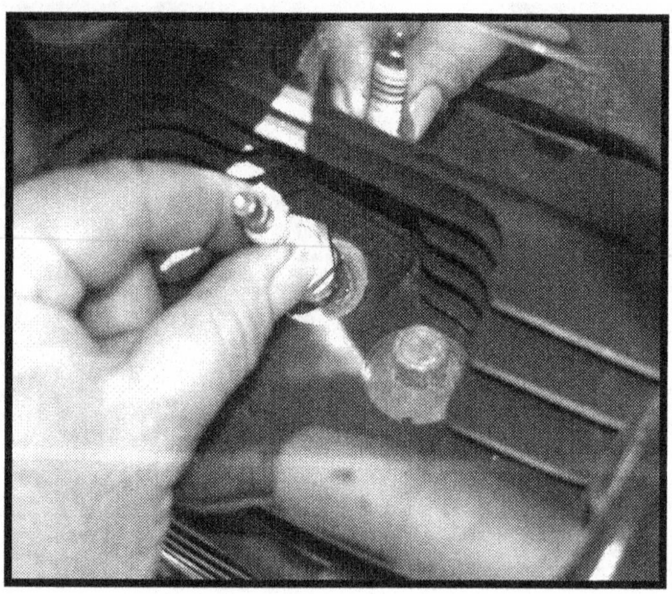

Fig. 74 Inserting Spark Plug by Hand

We have already gapped these new spark plugs and coated the threads with anti-seize compound and we can now install them, first by hand.

In Fig. 74, I am inserting the spark plugs without a wrench. I want to make absolutely certain the plug's threads are matching the cylinder head threads 100% perfectly. I am also going to insert the plug as far as I possibly can with my bare fingers.

After the plug binds up in the threads where I can't turn it anymore with my fingers, I will then apply the socket and turn the socket with my fingers, not using the wrench just yet, as shown in Fig. 71. I want to make sure the plug is going into the cylinder head deeply before applying any wrenching. This is how you prevent cross threading of threads. See Fig. 75. See the Notation on next page.

What if you do cross thread and ruin the threads? A Heli-coil can be inserted. It is a special repair device and tool that will install new threads. Better to have an experienced mechanic do that job for you, but you can do it yourself in some cases. Most of the time the cylinder head must be removed. Some kits can actually do it without removing the cylinder head because a few soft leftover aluminum chips in the cylinder will be expelled from the cylinder unlike steel chips that will not... you will be cutting aluminum, not steel to install a Heli-coil or using a tap to cut new threads.

Fig. 74 and Fig. 75 shows us inserting the spark plug by hand first then using a spark plug socket to turn by hand so threads will not become cross-threaded.

Note: Before applying the wrench look to see if the spark plug threads have descended all the way down into the cylinder head. It is best if you can get the threads all the way down by hand so that the crush washer is actually bottomed out against the cylinder head. This way it is safe to apply the wrench with no danger of cross-threading. If the plug is down only half way you must be very careful not to twist the spark plug sideways when screwing it down or the strong steel threads of the spark plug will tear into the soft aluminum cylinder head threads.

WHAT COMES NEXT?

Now that you have learned how to change the oil on your Harley Davidson motorcycle it is time to purchase a service manual. They are expensive and the manual may not cover everything you need to know, but it has a lot of good advice. It is a good place to begin your next journey into motorcycle repair as it will give you an understanding of procedure and the special tools you will need.

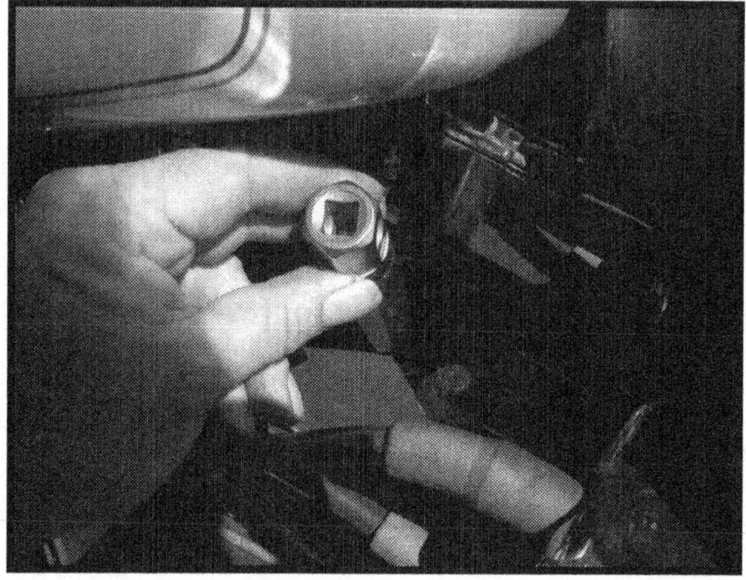

Fig. 75 Always Hand Tighten Spark Plugs First Before Using Wrench

UPGRADING BRAKES

Have you tried upgrading your brake pads to street competition brakes? You should try them. What you want is sintered metal pads for a cruiser motorcycle. Stock bikes have them, but the street competition pads are much more aggressive, yet very manageble for normal street and highway use.

Ask your Harley Davidson dealer to order you a set of DP brand pads or Ferodo brand pads. You will likely enjoy these brakes much once you get used to them. They have more stopping power, but they won't bite hard to lock-up the wheels under normal use. There are other brands you can choose from too.

Try a set of street competition brake pads. I have used them on my bikes with great success and they don't destroy the rotors.

Fig. 76 Do Not Bend the Spark Plug When Using a Wrench

What is wrong in Fig. 76? All seems well. The socket is deeply penetrating the spark plug, two fingers are gripping the wrench lightly to tighten the spark plug with light pressure. What could possibly be wrong?

Warning: there is no hand holding the top of the socket wrench ratchet section. This can create a bending force along with a turning force to be applied to the spark plug.

However, if we have screwed the spark plug in all the way down by hand, we are likely safe and okay. But let's not take chances. Let's do it right all of the time. Accidents here can be very expensive and troublesome. Use your other hand to make sure the force being applied by the wrench is a turning force only.

Warning: keep two fingers on the wrench when tightening. We only want the plug to be snug tight, not excessively tight. Over tightening will absolutely strip the threads!

Tightening Procedure: remember when we tightened those o-ring oil drain plugs how they felt when tightening them? They had that snug feeling, but they could be tightened a bit more until the plug finally stopped turning?

Well, these spark plugs will feel the same way. That metal gasket on the plug is called a crush-washer. As you tighten the plug it will feel like it is getting tight, but it is actually crushing the washer. Keep tightening about an inch or two more on the wrench handle and finally the plug will stop turning. At that point you are done. Do not try to tighten the plug anymore or you will risk stripping the threads.

Helpful Advice: you can use a torque wrench that will help you know for certain the nut or bolt is tight to specifications. Basically, for oil changing a torque wrench is not required.

We have finished this job.

Let's go on and learn how you can make your bike run better and last longer.

MOTORCYCLE MAGAZINES

There are many motorcycle magazines and you can learn a lot from reading them. Many of the articles can save you a lot of time and money.

Motorcycle test reviews seem to be a little more bent in favor of the manufacturer/advertiser, but often the article is fair, balanced overall.

Regardless, you need to speak to others who have the knowledge to get the entire story. By reading many magazines on the same subject you will get a much better understanding.

It really does pay you valuable benefits to purchase or subscribe to motorcycle magazines.

CHAPTER 7

ENGINE LONGEVITY TIPS

A late edition to this book; the tips in this engine longevity section should increase horsepower, reduce friction to extend engine life and increase fuel mileage. All are beneficial. Much advice has already been incorporated within the text in this book.

We have since revealed in Fig. 25 an engine oil filter magnet to trap fine abrasive metal filings.

Spark plugs and wires as shown in Fig. 61 and in Fig. 67 will increase horsepower and fuel mileage.

Read the next chapters (eight and nine) for more helpful advice as engine longevity tips have been incorporated there.

SHORTEST CHAPTER IN THE BOOK

It just happens that sometimes things don't go as planned and in this case the author simply decided to skip Chapter 7 by incorporating the elements of Chapter 7 into Chapter 8. It may not make sense to you and that's because it does not make sense to us either, but this is what makes life fun and interesting!

Also, we wanted the bragging rights to have the shortest book chapter in the history of motorcycling!

CHAPTER 8

PERPETUAL OIL CHANGE METHOD

This chapter alone should more than pay for the cost of this book in engine longevity!

Fig. 77 Removing Oil From Oil Tank

What is a perpetual oil change? You have likely never heard of this technique, but it is used with large industrial machinery that has hundreds of thousands of horsepower, like in huge gas and steam turbines in electric utilities, etc. This method is used in the tens of thousands of horsepower propulsion diesel engines in ocean going ships. That is how I learned about the perpetual oil change by working on power plant equipment when I was a steam power plant Engineer (read my book Steam & Diesel Power Plant Operators Examinations – answers for pre-employment and license exams).

I simplified and incorporated the method into motorcycles with great success. Your engine will last a lot longer than it normally would if otherwise you were using just the traditional oil change intervals. A traditional oil change permits the oil to gradually darken with “abrasive” impurities. That is what wears out your engine, circulating sandpaper-like laden oil to all engine friction surfaces. The perpetual oil change method keeps the oil super clean so abrasive action is greatly reduced to an absolute minimum.

There are many benefits to using this technique in your motorcycle. Let's go through the procedure on how quickly and easily it is performed, then later we can discuss the wonderful things it will do for your engine. This method can be performed on any motorcycle and it is not a dirty job and takes only a few minutes to do!

ENGINE OIL SWEETENING PROCEDURE

Fig. 77 reveals the motorcycle is on the side stand. No need to put the bike up on a lift. We are using a simple automotive battery sponge-bulb to suck out the oil in the oil tank. We have a 2-cup plastic cup (known also as a 16 ounce party cup). Keep removing the oil and place it in this plastic cup as is shown in Fig. 78.

Note: on some motorcycles you can use a simple siphon hose to remove oil from the engine crankcase.

Fig. 78 Easy and Clean Job

When the cup is filled put it aside and then fill a second cup with old oil from the oil tank. We only want to remove 32 ounces (2 party cups). Put these two cups aside where they will not be accidentally knocked over.

Better yet, pour the oil into some empty oil containers, throw away the two old party cups and recycle the used oil at a oil reclamation station (usually where you purchased the oil or at a auto parts store).

Now get another new 16 ounce plastic cup and fill it with new oil and pour the oil into the oil tank as shown in Fig. 79.

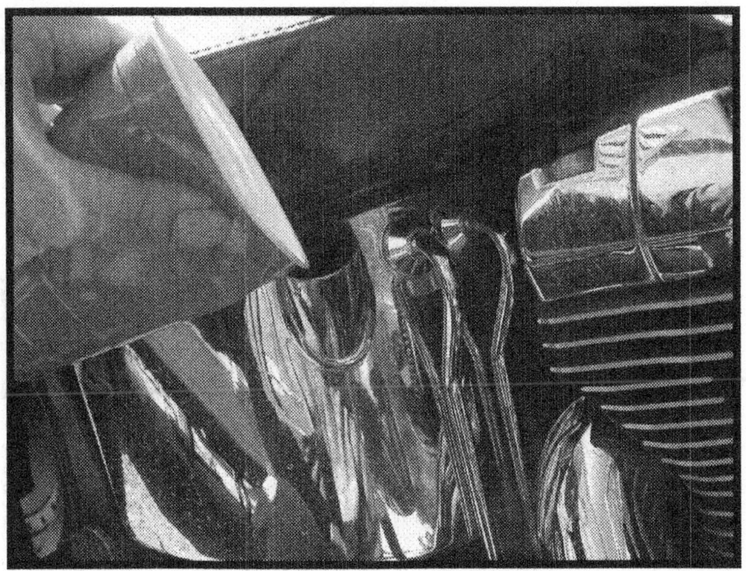

Fig. 79 Pouring New Oil In Oil Tank

Fig. 79 shows us adding 16 fluid ounces of new oil to the oil tank. Now add 8-fluid ounce of new oil (halfway point in the cup) into the plastic cup and add the rest of the way with Duralube (or another reputable brand) oil additive (additive added is optional or substitute with normal or synthetic motor oil). See Fig. 81. Then pour this 16-fluid ounce cup into the oil tank. We have now replaced the same amount of oil we have removed.

Sometimes I just use an ordinary 8 ounce Styrofoam drinking cup and add that amount of "oil additive" to the engine. It's all a Twin Cam engine really needs to be fully protected. See Fig. 80.

Note: you can use plastic or glass measuring cups if you wish, but I find that using the disposable cups easier to use as there is no cleaning of the measuring cups and there is no chance of contaminates entering the oil from an oil dampened dirt-laden measuring cup.

Fig. 80 - An 8 ounce Styrofoam Cup

Yes, you can blend the normal engine oil with modern synthetic oil and still add 8-fluid ounce of Duralube additive to have a triple blend of oil. As long as the viscosity and API ratings of the oils match for the intended service there will be no problem. Duralube is an oil lubricant enhancer for your Harley Davidson Twin Cam engine. The viscosity is less than 20-50 weight, but we are only adding a small amount of 8-ounces to the mix. It will not harm anything as this lower viscosity oil quiets the valve lifters and reduces other engine noise.

Note: I have used 8 ounces of Duralube additive in motorcycles that use one-single-oil for the engine, primary and transmission with no problems. It will not cause the clutch to slip. However, I do not use it or any other additives in the Harley Davison transmission. I do use it in the Harley Davidson primary chain case with no problems, just add ¼ cup of the Styrofoam cup (2 ounces) as shown in Figure 80. It should protect your primary case components from excessive wear and tear and should quiet down chain and clutch-related noises.

You may notice that by adding Duralube additive (or other reputable brand of friction reducing oil) the engine valve train noise will be reduced, acceleration and more power is now available and fuel mileage increases. It should make your engine last a long time. The cams and bearing and the cam followers should not wear down as fast as would using normal oil change intervals. Heat should not harm your engine if it is much better protected.

Here's the formula: add this formula to the engine oil (engine only, not transmission or primary case).

ENGINE OIL FORMULA

Add 8-fluid ounce of normal oil (1/2 of a 16 ounce cup).
Add 16-fluid ounce synthetic SNY3 oil (full 16 ounce cup).
Add 8-fluid ounce of Duralube additive (1/2 of a 16 ounce cup).

The above engine oil formula is only for the perpetual oil change method. Do not use it for the normal scheduled oil change.

You can use the below formulas for the primay case and transmission in the normal scheduled oil change.

PRIMARY CHAIN CASE FORMULA

Add 1 quart of synthetic SNY3 oil.
Add 2-fluid ounce of Duralube additive (1/2 of a 16 ounce cup).

TRANSMISSION FORMULA

Add ¾ quart of synthetic SNY3 oil.

No additive is used in the transmission. If Harley Davidson one day decides to make a transmission additive, then use it.

OIL ADDITIVES

If Duralube additive is not available look for a similar oil additive using no solid particles like Teflon or molybdenum, or whatever, suspended in the oil. Just find a pure lubricant friction-reducing product. Or simply forget about using oil additives and just switch to pure synthetic oil or use a blend of regular oil with synthetic.

Some bikes may not be able to use friction decreasing additives as the engine oil is also used to wet the clutch. Trial and error will let you know if you can use it or not. Just add a little bit of additive and see what happens. You can also contact the manufacturer and ask for their advice as that would be the best method to employ.

There are many conflicts of opinion out there pertaining to oil and most of them are just plain fantasy. **Example**: people blamed the new synthetic oils on bearing failure on some motorcycles, but it was not the oil. It was later discovered by the manufacturer the bearing itself was defective and would fail in any oil. Now the manufacturer puts synthetic oil in all of their bike engines. Get the point? Oil will not destroy your engine as long as the API rating on the oil container matches the manufactures recommended API service rating.

Oil additives when used in small amounts will not destroy your engine. The best oil additive will simply be a lubricant with no solid particles. Duralube and Marvel Mystery Oil additives are like that. They have no solid particles to accumulate to clog oil passageways or change engine clearances. However, read the product label as I have no control if they change the formula after I write this book. More new high-tech products are being developed all of the time. You may even find a better product to use. I bet we will too!

That is why I don't use Teflon based additives, but you can use them if you wish at least in motorcycles that have a separate wet clutch oil compartment like in the Twin Cam engine Harley Davidson has. Just don't use them in the wet clutch compartment. Use them in the engine oil only. Again, to be fair, Harley Davidson does not recommend using oil additives in their engines. Using a high grade of synthetic oil in place of adding the oil additive may even be better for your engine.

Okay, let us now talk about the benefits of the perpetual oil change method.

Fig. 81 Example of a Friction Reducing Oil Additive.

What we have just done is sweeten the oil in the engine. Now what do you think is better an engine with 1,000 miles on it with no oil change or an engine with 1,000 miles on it but half the oil is new? And a portion of that new oil has anti-wear additive enhancements?

PERPETUAL OIL CHANGE

It really works! It works to the benefit of your motorcycle and it can extend the oil change intervals as long as you desire in many cases to exceed the recommended oil changes.

Let's assume you want to extend your scheduled oil change to each 10,000 miles instead of 2,500 miles. You simply keep replacing and adding oil each week, or each 300 miles. By using the Perpetual Oil Change method the oil will never become dirty.

The oil has to stay clean because the oil is perputaally being changed, little by little, each 300 miles. If the oil is clean the oil filter will not need changing as often, so it can go 10,000 miles with ease.

If your motor is old with high miles and tends to foul the engine oil the Perpetual Oil Change method will be ideal for you, but since the oil is always being contaminated at a rapid rate in an old engine, you should change the oil filter each 2,500 miles just to be on the safe side of things.

CHAPTER 9

HELPFUL ADVICE

FUEL ADDITIVES

Think about it. If you do this each 1,000 miles the oil will not need to be changed for a long time. That is how they run those big million-horsepower steam and gas turbines for years on end, month upon months without stopping to change the oil. They keep draining a bit and adding fresh oil so the oil always stays relatively clean all of the time. Get the picture? The oil is always being changed, little by little.

If you keep draining a portion of the oil, say each 500 miles, the oil has no chance to become dark colored and filled with abrasive soot and contaminating acids, etc. The oil is always cleaner in this motorcycle engine than the person who waits and changes the oil when he hits 2.500 miles or more. Half the time the engine is running on dirty abrasive-laden oil before it gets changed with clean oil only to become dirty again all too soon. This dirty oil cycle wears out the engine 100% faster!

How long does it take to perform a perpetual oil change? Just a few minutes and there are no wrenches, no drain pan or a toolbox full of tools required. It is fast, clean and efficient plus you can keep on going without having to stop for an oil change when traveling on a road trip.

Now, you should still change your engine oil and oil filter. After about four perpetual oil changes, each at about 700 to 1,000 miles (2,800 or 4,000 miles) it is time to perform a full oil and oil filter change. Drain the oil and change the oil filter as you normally would do. All we are doing is extending the miles between scheduled oil changes without damaging the engine and keeping the oil cleaner than it would be between normal oil changes. Clean oil will give you a long lasting engine, no doubt about that!

You can set your own formula and time intervals for changing your oil. What I have given is just a technique that I have used in my Harley Davidson Twin Cam engine with very great success with zero engine problems at 56,000 miles. No bearing failures, no cam chain tension follower failures, no oil leaks, no abnormal or loud engine noise, etc. A perfectly true-running engine.

Keeping the engine oil clean keeps the bottom end clean, but only fuel additives can clean and lubricate the valves, piston rings and domes and cylinder head areas.

Oil carbon builds up as oil vapors are circulated into the air intake breather system to be burned inside the cylinders. This creates carbon to accumulate on the piston and valves.

Detonation occurs even when not heard as knocks and pings begin to hammer, shake, shock and crack the piston rings. The carbon also builds up along the piston ring grooves and the valve stems and guides where this brittle carbon acts like sandpaper wearing the cylinders and valves way before their time.

Also, overfilling the engine oil compartment creates more oil vapors to enter the engine speeding up the carbon building process. Carbon will build up due to normal use and anti-smog control devices.

Adding gasoline fuel additives to the gasoline tank will dissolve much of these carbon deposits and keep them to a minimal level. It will also remove the power robbing carbon deposits that foul the piston rings and this will give you more power all of the time.

Carbon not only robs power but it destroys your engine prematurely. Premium fuel often has detergents to improve carbon cleaning, but a good healthy dose of over-the-counter fuel treatment will clear out the tough deposits premium gasoline can't remove.

Fig. 82 reveals a fuel additive made by Lucas that can give your bike's engine a new life and keep it that way for a very long time. It can do a lot

HARSH CHEMICALS

Some fuel additives can be too aggressive and harm fuel system rubber seals. It is best to use additives when touring so the additive can't sit in the tank for hours or days. For best results just add the chemical and burn it off quickly.

for your engine. Read the bottle and you will see just how beneficial it is. You can also use Marvel Mystery Oil in your gas tank if you want to. I like to use Lucas Upper Cylinder Lubricant or Marvel Mystery Oil. Lucas is a big supporter of top fuel NHRA drag racing.

Yes, there are and will be other gasoline additives and lubricants available now or in the future. Go ahead and try them. The point is this. It can be better to use additives to help clean and lubricate an engine than to not use them at all. Gasoline you buy already has additives so you know they are needed and they do work.

Fig. 82 Gasoline Additive

Note: Some oil additives that are used in motor oil can be too slippery or may have elements that can cause the wet clutch in a motorcycle to slip. The Twin Cam motor has a separate primary chain & clutch case, so just don't use additives in this compartment unless you know it is okay to use them.

What to do if the clutch slips after adding an additive? Drain the oil from the primary case and replace with Harley Davidson primary case oil.

Fig. 83 One Shot, Please

A shot glass holds about ¼ fluid ounce. Just a short pour will do the trick. You don't need a lot of additive in the gasoline, so less is better than more.

Many of these multipurpose gasoline additives can be added to the engine oil too, but I don't use them for that purpose. I like to use specific products for a specific purpose in my engines.

Note: Harley Davidson does sell its own brand of gasoline additives. You should use them.

The oil base additives like, Lucas and Marvel, can raise the heat content of fuel to give you more miles per gallon along with a power boost.

Warning: more fuel additive is not better. The engine is designed to run on gasoline. Too much additive can actually foul the spark plugs or prevent the gas from burning and the engine will not run. Just use a small amount of gasoline additive. Read the product label for the recommended amount.

How often should you use a gasoline additive? All of the time, each time you fill your gas tank if you wish. This way everything inside the engine cylinder stays clean.

Octane boosting additives can help prevent cylinder detonation by raising the octane level in your gas tank, especially when using single-hose gasoline pumps that dispense a quart of low octane regular gasoline before premium fuel appears. The single-hose gas station pump "dilutes" your gas tank's octane, yet you still paid premium prices for that inferior gas.

SAFE ADDITIVES

Additives such as Lucas and Marvel Mystery Oil as described in this book are not aggressive and are safe to use and to leave in the fuel tank for days or weeks. That is because they are oil-based and contain no volitile alcohols, napthas or other harsh and aggressive chemicals.

What may be safe to use in a car engine may not be safe to use in a motorcycle. This is another good reason to read motorcycle magazines as they will often tell you which products are safe to use.

I most all cases, it is always safe to use Harley Davidson additives in your Harley Davidson motorcycle, but you should still read the product label instructions and consider not leaving the additive in the gas tank for more than a day.

NEW CAM CHAIN TENSION SYSTEM

The new Dyna engine for model year 2006 has new larger cam bearings, a revised cam chain and hydralic tensioning system. This will fix many problems, but you still need to keep an eye on those Nylon-type cam follower shoes. They can still wear out over time, but they should not wear out as fast as there is much less tension on the shoes with this fix.

There are some general flaws in the Twin Cam engine you need to be aware of. This is why I strongly recommend that Twin Cam (Dyna's, etc.) all use synthetic oil as it will extend your engine life greatly and to use the perpetual oil change method listed in this book. The cleaner the oil, the more lubricity it will have and all the more cooler the engine will run.

Cams: there once was a cam bearing failure problem, but it has been fixed, but as of this writing the cam bearings are being replaced with larger bearings (starting with the Dyna model motorcycle in the year 2006). The Twin Cam engine may be updated at a later date. Once in awhile a camshaft "roller bearing" fails and it can lead to serious engine destruction. It is important that you listen to your engine and try to detect strange noises as soon as possible. If you hear a strange noise, get the engine inspected right away.

Cam Chain: There is a problem with the cam chain tension shoes wearing out. These Nylon-type fiber shoes keep the cam chain tight. When the shoes wear out the chain will flap and make serious noise with devastating engine destruction. Sometimes the shoes just self-destruct in a moment without warning. See new system box on page 124.

You will hear a grinding and rattling sound near the timing cover and push rods (right side of the engine). It is the steel chain grinding aluminum and steel metal inside your engine. The motor can be destroyed, but in many cases it can be salvaged if the metal chips did not migrate throughout the engine and if the chain does not break or grind up too many things it its path.

This is a weakness in the Twin Cam engine that can lead to catastrophic engine failure. Eventually, these shoes will fail on your engine. The question is when will it happen? Next month? Next year? Tomorrow?

There is an aftermarket kit available that removes the chain system and replaces them with gears. This would be a good investment if you plan to keep a camshaft roller bearing Twin Cam engine for maximum miles and service, especially when touring long distances.

Important: every motorcycle manufacturer has inherent weak points in their motorcycles, so please do not think that Harley Davidson is unique in this regards. There is no perfect motorcycle.

If you ever have your bike in a reputable shop ask them to inspect the cam chain shoes and replace them if need be every 25,000 miles or less. It is an expensive inspection but necessary once your original or extended warrantee has expired. If you can't afford to do this, then just listen to your engine each day being intent on finding a new sounding noise to identify trouble. Loud engine exhaust will absolutely prevent detection. Place the rounded handle of a screwdriver to your hear and the screwdriver blade on the engine case. This will help detect unusual sounds. But, a visual inspection is the only reliable method to prevent an unexpected engine failure.

Note: If you are paying to have the inspection you may as well replace the shoes anyway with new ones. If you calculate the cost of inspections and shoe replacement it may be cheaper (and with great peace of mind gained) to switch to the gear drive system. Ask your Harley Davidson dealer's mechanic for advice, they may have a fix for this problem.

Piston & Valve Wear: The top end is weak in the Twin Cam engine. Most all air-cooled engines have this wear problem. The pistons and valves are hot and bake in the heat so they wear out faster than the bottom-end components, primary or transmission. You can use fuel and oil additives to greatly extend, even double the longevity of the engine.

To help avoid the above engine failures using superior lubrication oil and fuel treatment can be a great asset.

OIL COOLING

It is my opinion every air-cooled engine should automatically come with the oil cooler as standard equipment. The oil must lubricate and also cool the engine. The oil is hotter than the metal inside the engine (in most areas) and the thermostat controlled external air-cooled oil cooler is a must have to manage engine temperatures. High temperature will kill and engine fast and the top end of Harley Davidson air-cooled motorcycle engines really do need that oil cooler, or else! Install an oil cooler right away and it will save your engine from an early self-destruction.

Note: Make sure you tell the mechanic to watch the torque when installing the oil cooler adapter mount to the engine case. The soft rubber gasket can easily expand into the oil case hole cutting the oil flow in half! Sheet rubber is not a good choice here. A standard gasket or O-ring that will not migrate would have been a better fitment, but soft flowing sheet rubber gasket is what the aftermarket or OEM manufacturer usually sends with the oil cooler components.

Contrary to popular belief you do not need to carry a large volume of tools on a motorcycle. Most riders only need the list below. Others will need more because they have problems with their bike that they alone know about that occur with frequency.

Some riders never carry flat tire repair kits as they do not know how to use them. Carry one anyway. Somebody else or a mechanic nearby likely does know how, but does not have the tools and parts to help you. Now he will!

Example: any automotive repair garage or nearby mechanic can fix a flat tire if you have the specialized tools and specific parts for him to use.

The adjustable wrench will fit many nuts and bolts on the bike, not just loosen axle nuts. A spare spark plug will bail you out if bad fuel or carbon fouls a plug. You can carry two spares if you wish. Pliers will remove metal nails from tires, etc.

1. Spare spark plug.
2. An electrical fuse kit with the correct amperage fuses for your bike.
3. Spark plug socket and a wrench to turn the socket.
4. Flat tire repair kit for tubeless tires (with four CO2 air cylinders to inflate tire).
5. Three tire irons and one tube repair kit if you have spoke wheels.
6. Normal size needle-nose pliers.
7. Large adjustable wrench that will fit front and rear axle nuts.

8. Flathead and a Philips screwdriver.
9. Small LED flashlight for night repairs.
10. Spare headlight bulb (if it is not a sealed beam light).
11. Tail and turn signal light bulbs.
12. Plastic electrical tape is handy for all sorts of things.
13. Motorcycle jumper cables. Someday you will wish you had them!
14. Spool of wire to jump failed electrical parts, even to hotwire a headlight if need be.
15. Any tools to access expected failed items. Socket, box, Allen wrench, etc.
16. Any other tools you know will be needed for your bike.

It can be handy to have one of those "All-In-One" tools that seem to have everything on them spreads into a fan-like display. You can get them at any hardware store. The only drawback is that the tools often do not have a long reach, so don't rely 100% on this tool.

Before an emergency failure occurs make sure all of the tools and parts fit properly and will function before you store them away in your carry-on tool pouch. If you need a 10mm or a 9/16" wrench to access an area and don't have that wrench with you, your entire tool kit is nonfunctional.

VALVE LASH ADJUSTMENTS

We all know Twin Cam and other Harley Davidson engines do not need scheduled valve adjustments because they use hydraulic lifters. Think again! The Harley Davidson V-rod engine needs valve lash adjusting and it is not inexpensive to perform as the engine needs to be removed from the frame just to get access to the valves. Other motorcycle manufactureres are doing this too, so make sure you ask the right questions before buying a new motorcycle. Some bikes require a valve adjustment each 7,000 miles and that can be expensive to operate and inconvenient.

We have a free checklist you can print out from our Website http://www.JamesRussellPublishing.com

This checklist will ask all the right questions for you and help you to get the best deal too. It is free. Just click on our motorcycle section. Print some out and give them to your friends and riding club members. We have useful motorcycle articles for you to read, all for free. We also have motorcycle books and motorcycle movies too.

NO SKINNY FRONT TIRES

Be aware that it may look cool to have a skinny 21" front tire on your motorcycle, but it makes for a very rough ride and it can be dangerous.

HOW?

The small tire diameter can catch easily into imperfections in the pavement and this will create a struggle for the driver to just ride the bike normally, fighting the road. It can tire you out in no time at all.

Another problem is that the 21" wheel can actually get caught in a deep groove in the pavement and yank the handlebar right out of your hands, or cause a crash from instant deceleration.

You need to consider that the bikes with those large 16" front tires are not only safer, but are much smoother on the road and much more tollerant of defects in roadways.

Yes, the 21" wheel looks great, but they are not practical in the real world if you plan on riding your motorcycle a lot. Your Harley Davidson dealer can upgrade your 21" to a 19" wheel or better yet the 16" wheel.

The 16" wheel has a solid fat diameter that places a much larger contact patch on the roadway. It will slip a lot less than that skinny 21" wheel when driving through sand, fuel or oil spills or other small objects in the roadway.

CHAPTER 10

A FEW WORDS FROM THE AUTHOR

I hope you enjoyed this book and I wish you many safe rides. Every time a biker dies from a survivable accident by not wearing a helmet with body armor it is sad.

I have switched to a full-face helmet and wear riding clothing with body armor some years ago. It is not so cool-looking to be dead. I see too many die at the motorcycle rallies and in every town and city on a daily basis that would have survived otherwise. Yes, it is a personal choice. Why not choose to live so you can ride another day?

Have you read any books on how to ride safely? You should. I rode for many years and I was shocked to discover how much of a sitting duck I was in traffic when I read a motorcycle instruction book for the first time. It has saved me on many occasions already from serious accidents from cars and road objects. We have these books on our Website, so go check them out. Believe me you will really appreciate me telling you about these books once you get one in your hand.

Also, if you are going to ride motorcycles you are likely to die on one, but regardless you will die one day... statistics have proven that one out of one will die, that is 100%. Have you thought where you will spend eternity? When you visit our Website we have a Christian section you should visit so you can get right with God while you still can. We also have many free gifts we wish to give you, so come visit us.

FREE TOUR MAPS

We have very interesting motorcycle rally tour maps you will not find on ordinary road maps. We will show you places to see things you have never seen before… and it is free! The maps are also good for cars too!

Our Website has free self-guided tour maps you can print out. Yes, we do have unique and fun tours for the Black Hills Sturgis Rally, Spearfish Canyon and Mt. Rushmore in South Dakota. The Laughlin River Run Rally and Reno Street Vibrations motorcycle rallies too! in Nevada, etc. You will really like these free tours. Tell your friends! Come experience something new!

A FREE GOLD COIN

We even have a free gold-tone biker coin to give you while supplies last. This coin is way better than those good-luck bells you see hanging on motorcycles. Come to our Website and get a free sample! http://www.JamesRussellPublishing.com

VISIT OUR WEBSITE

For free gifts, motorcycle books, motorcycle rally tour guide books, biker movies, useful links, also helpful motorcycle articles and articles on many other subjects are available free of charge. Just type James Russell Publishing into any Internet search engine to find us.

http://www.JamesRussellPublishing.com

TELL YOUR RIDING FRIENDS TO VISIT OUR WEBSITE

Internet Address Book

The Book Every Computer Needs!

PROFESSIONAL VERSION!

Cover Price 19.95. ISBN 0-916367-12-6. 118pp., 8x11 format.

If you have a computer you need this book. The Internet Address Book is two books in one. A book to maintain Internet contacts and a log book for recording critical CMOS & BIOS computer files and software specifications.

No address book can match the data saving convienience to the computer user like the Internet Address Book can. Once a computer owner uses this book they will not compute without it!

Put this book on your computer bookshelf and see how fast it sells. The book is exactly what every Internet surfer needs... a handy book to record Web site data.

Read what this book can do...

You can wait until your computer fails and lose your Internet and computer data or you can save yourself a ton of grief and buy this book now! **James Russell - Author**

* * * *

This book is available in paperback and as an e-book. You will not be disappointed!

SHIPPING

NOW!

ORDER TODAY!

THE MARKET IS HUGE

Telephone address books can be found everywhere, but now comes the Internet Address Book!

Just about everyone who owns a computer surfs the Internet and most all suffer from forgetting passwords, software and hardware failure, losing CD-Key numbers, e-mail addresses, you name it. This is the book to solve these problems.

There are no Internet Address Books 100% dedicated to the general Website surfer and the professional business-person... until now!

FEATURES

- Log Internet Website addresses.
- Record computer data to prevent data loss.
- Never forget another password or ID number to enter any Website.
- Record Internet contact and e-mail addresses and even manage sites linking to your Website.
- Safegard Internet data even if your computer is stolen.
- Log your software preferences and CD-Key numbers.
- Recover from virus attacking CMOS or BIOS configurations.
- Supports up to six computers.
- Supports 50 Websites.
- Suports 30 software programs.
- Reover from Internet data loss.

J R P

PUBLISHER DISCOUNTS
Bookstore Spec. Order 20%
Individuals $19.95
S & H $4 single copy.

PUBLISHER – SAN 295-852X
James Russell Publishing
www.JamesRussellPublishing.com

DISTRIBUTORS
Baker & Taylor (800)775-1100
www.btol.com
Ingrams (800)937-8000
www.ingram.com

Trap Shooting Secrets

Endorsed by Professional Shooters

THE FIRST TRAP SHOOTING TECHNICAL BOOK!

Cover Price 34.95. ISBN 0-916367-09-6. 183pp., 8x11 format, over 85 technical illustrations.

There has never been a book like this, ever! *TSS* is like having a shooting coach telling you precisely what to do to hit the targets. In fact, the book is so effective, it is the only book ever to be endorsed by professional trapshooters who make a living in the shooting sports and their testimonials are on the back cover!

Books have been published on trap shooting, but not one has ever been written as a true technical textbook giving detailed step-by-step instructions to shoot high scores. This book turns mediocre shooters into winning champions! The author has performed numerous interviews with the pros to discover the inner secrets and winning ways of the game and has successfully communicated this intangible subject into a powerful book that gives readers results!

I strongly recommend shotgun competition shooters read both Trap Shooting Secrets and Precision Shooting - The Trapshooter's Bible ***Luca Scribani Rossi*** **– Olympic Medallist & Team Coach.**

* * * *

The concepts in these two books are strongly presented and easily applied. Valuable advice! ***Daro Handy – Hall of Fame Professional Trap Shooter***

SHIPPING

NOW!

ORDER TODAY!

THE MARKET IS HUGE

Trap shooting is a hidden sport. In the USA there are over 150, 000 extremely dedicated registered trapshooters who compete for money and prizes. Triple that figure for the world.

Wing shooters discovered the book invaluable to hitting targets and they number at **8.5 million**! This book, with it's follow-on companion book, ***Precision Shooting - The Trapshooters Bible*** are very fast movers in bookstores, often sold the first day displayed on the shelf! Visit our Website to read superb customer testimonials! Order today.

You Won't Be Disappointed!

FEATURES

- Powerful clay target shooting instructions. Secrets of the pros.
- All phases of shooting covered; equipment, concentration, form technique and valuable tips.
- Over 85 illustrations reveals the inner *secrets* of the game.
- Small talk eliminated. The book gets right to the facts and goes deep fast and stays there!
- Professionals have never endorsed any target shooting books prior to this book! That's over 150 years! Endorsed by shooting magazines!
- Readers are given strong instructions, accurate advice and over 135 practice tips they can use immediately! Even videotapes can't match the power and effectiveness of this book! A best-seller!

PUBLISHER DISCOUNTS
Bookstore Spec. Order 20%
Individuals $34.95
S & H $4 single copy.

PUBLISHER – SAN 295-852X
James Russell Publishing
www.JamesRussellPublishing.com

DISTRIBUTORS
Baker & Taylor (800)775-1100
www.btol.com
Ingrams (800)937-8000
www.ingram.com

Precision Shooting - The Trapshooter's Bible

For Professional Shooters

...AND THOSE WHO WANT TO BE!

This is the follow-on book of *Trap Shooting Secrets* and it's

Better Than Ever!

...**Now the *only* trap shooting book with ATA and Olympic-style Double-Trap technical instructions with illustrations!**

...**The *only* professional advanced-level trap shooting book in the world!**

...**Proven winning how-to advice for shotgun competition shooters!**

...**The *only* clay target shooting book with hundreds of answers to technical shooting questions answered in great detail!**

...**Endorsed by *professional* shotgun shooting instructors!**

...**Readers obtain high-score *results* with *Precision Shooting*!**

Cover Price 34.95. ISBN 0-916367-10X. 220pp., 8x11 format, over 145 technical illustrations, plus 315 questions & answers!

I strongly recommend shotgun competition shooters read both Trap Shooting Secrets and Precision Shooting - The Trapshooter's Bible ***Luca Scribani Rossi*** **– Olympic Medallist & Team Coach**

* * * *

The concepts in these two books are strongly presented and easily applied. Valuable advice! ***Daro Handy – Hall of Fame Professional Trap Shooter***

SHIPPING

NOW!

ORDER TODAY!

THE ULTIMATE

Presicion Shooting **and *Trap Shooting Secrets* are endorsed by highly acclaimed qualified pro shooters, instructors and shooting magazines!**

No other shotgun shooting books compare with these two books. Why? Because these are the only technical textbooks ever written for the sport and they deliver on the promise!

These books don't talk about shooting, they are comprehensive show-me-how-to-shoot instructional books, like have a shooting coach by your side showing you what to do!

The shotgun books you have on your shelves pale in comparison in regards to effectiveness and fast sales!

Visit our Website to read superb customer testimonials! Order today.

You Won't Be Disappointed!

FEATURES

- Reveals the secrets professionals use to hit targets with consistent accuracy!
- All phases of shooting covered; equipment, concentration, form technique and valuable tips.
- Over 145 illustrations reveals the inner *secrets* of the game.
- More than 315 answers to tough target shooting questions!
- This is no small book. 220 pp in large 8X11 format jammed with shotgun shooting instructions!
- Readers are stunned to discover the secrets of clay target shootisng revealed. Professionals witheld these secrets to maintain their winning edge, but now all is shed to light! Wing shooters love this book!
- #1 best-seller in the sport!

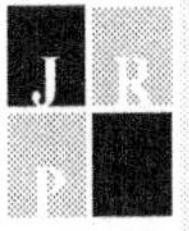

PUBLISHER DISCOUNTS
Bookstore Spec. Order 20%
Individuals $34.95
S & H $4 single copy.

PUBLISHER – SAN 295-852X
James Russell Publishing
www.JamesRussellPublishing.com

DISTRIBUTORS
Baker & Taylor Phone: (800)775-1100
www.btol.com
Ingrams (800)937-8000
www.ingram.com

Screen & Stage Marketing Secrets

100% Dedicated To Selling Scripts

THE ONLY SCRIPT MARKETING BOOK!

Cover Price 34.95. ISBN 0-916367-11-8. 180pp., 8x11 format, over 40 technical illustrations.

There are many books on how to write a screenplay, teleplay or stage play script, but only this book tells you how to get your script sold! Step by step instructions are given to perform the marketing process. No theory here, just show-me-how-to-do-it advice!

Writing a script is hard, it's even harder to sell it. *Screen & Stage Marketing Secrets* is an invaluable tool to insure scripts are presented professionally. Rejections will be vastly reduced. All marketing procedures are covered. There are even sample query and cover letters the writer can use. Script marketing is not taught in film schools, now it will be!

More than 200,000 scripts are submitted each year to Hollywood and Broadway and most are rejected due to improper marketing. For decades there has been a dire need for this book. Here it is!

I was surprised to discover just how much I learned. This book is valuable! ***Zeolot - Screenwriter***

* * * *

Their should be a book so writers can learn how to submit scripts professionally. This is it! ***Literary Agent***

* * * *

Everything you need to know to market your screenplay, TV or stage play script - James R.

SHIPPING

NOW!

ORDER TODAY!

THE MARKET

Every major bookstore stocks screenwriting books since most schools offer theater and film courses. That means writers everywhere need this book to get their scripts sold!

This is the *only* technical book 100% dedicated to marketing screenplays, stage plays and television scripts!

Writers will find *Screen & Stage Marketing Secrets* of great value!

Visit our Website to read superb customer testimonials! Order today.

Satisfaction Guaranteed!

FEATURES

- Get an agent or sell your script without one!
- Write powerful and responsive query and cover letters!
- Avoid scriptwriting mistakes!
- Obtain high response from literary agencies!
- Contact production companies without an agent!
- Contact movie stars!
- Get more requests for your scripts!
- Present your scripts professionally to get them sold!
- Access the movie, television and stage play market!
- List of agents willing to give readers of this book *special consideration*! And much more!

PUBLISHER DISCOUNTS
Bookstore Spec. Order 20%
Individuals $34.95
S & H $4 single copy.

PUBLISHER - **SAN 295-852X**
James Russell Publishing
JamesRussellPublishing.com

DISTRIBUTORS
Baker & Taylor (800)775-1100
www.btol.com
Ingrams (800)937-8000
www.ingram.com

Steam & Diesel Power Plant Operators Exams

1,400 TEST QUESTIONS & ANSWERS!

STEAM & DIESEL
POWER PLANT
OPERATORS
EXAMINATIONS
JAMES RUSSELL

Cover Price 34.95. ISBN 0-916367-08-8. 117pp., 8x11 format, over 1,400 questions & answers.

There are numerous power plants in every city in the world and employees must learn how to operate the machinery. This is the book giving the correct answers to operate a power plant safely.

Stationary engineer boiler operators must pass pre-employment exams, and in some locations licensing exams. This is a powerful book giving readers the results they need... to get hired!

Other steam plant operations books can't measure up to the sheer volume of critical questions & answers in this book. However, this book goes beyond other technical books giving readers "explanations" as to why the answer to the question is correct. This book has been a bestseller to the power plant industry since 1981.

EXAMPLE

Boiler Water Total Dissolved Solids are High. You Should...

A. Increase Sulfite Chemical.

B. Increase steam drum surface blow.

C. Add Sulfite chemical to dearetor.

D. Decrease surface blow & perform - A.

E. Answers A & C is to be implemented.

F. Add calcium chloride to boilder water.

Correct Answer is "B".

SHIPPING

NOW!

ORDER TODAY!

A STRONG MARKET

Power plants are everywhere. You can use this book to score high on power plant exams!

Civil Service exams must be taken for those entering the stationary engineering field. This book has the answers to score high!

Oil refineries, food processing, electronic firms, metal fabrication mills, electric generating stations and hospitals, military bases all need this book for employee training!

Order today.

You won't be disappointed!

FEATURES

1. 1,400 questions & answers in multiple choice format.

2. You will learn the proper operational procedures and know why they are performed to enhance the safety of yourself and your fellow employees.

A. Many subjects are covered: Steam turbines, boilers, feed pumps, deareators, superheaters, steam engines, cooling tower, refrigeration, cutting in boilers and taking them off the line and much more!

B. Basic stationary emergency electrical generator diesel engines for ship-to-shore power and emergency power for hospitals are included.

C. Even steam engines are covered!

D. Every subject about power plant operations is covered from starting and shutting down boilers and equipment... safely!

PUBLISHER DISCOUNTS
Bookstore Spec. Order 20%
Individuals $34.95
S & H $4 single copy.

PUBLISHER – SAN 295-852X
James Russell Publishing
www.JamesRussellPublishing.com

DISTRIBUTORS
Baker & Taylor (800)775-1100
www.btol.com
Ingrams (800)937-8000
www.ingram.com

JAMES RUSSELL
PUBLISHING
BOOK CATALOG

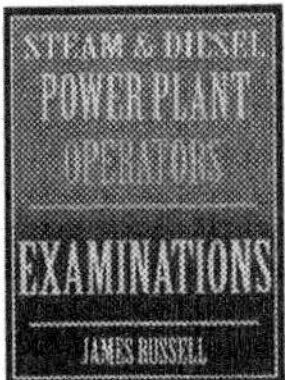

STEAM & DIESEL POWER PLANT OPERATORS EXAMINATIONS

ISBN-10: 0-916367-08-8 ISBN-13: 978-0-916367- 08-4

117 pp., 8x11, illustrated, $34.95 Over 1,400 multiple-choice test questions & answers (with explanations) helps stationary engineer power plant operators pass steam boiler licensing and pre-employment exams. This book has the answers to the exams!

TRAP SHOOTING SECRETS

ISBN-10: 0-916367-09-6 ISBN-13: 978-0-916367- 09-1

18-3 pp., 8x11, 85 illustrations, $34.95. There has never been a book like this, ever! *TSS* is like having a shooting coach telling you precisely what to do to hit the targets. It is the first book ever to be endorsed by professional trap shooters!

PRECISION SHOOTING - THE TRAPSHOOTER'S BIBLE

ISBN-10: 0-916367-10-X ISBN-13: 978-0-916367-10-7

230 pp., 8x11, 145 illustrations, $34.95. The *only* trap shooting book with ATA & Olympic Double-Trap technical instructions. The *only* professional advanced-level trapshooting book in the world. Has hundreds of answers to competition shooting questions in great detail to help you understand precisely what professional shooters know.

SCREEN & STAGE MARKETING SECRETS

ISBN-10: 0-916367-11-8 ISBN-13: 978-0-916367-11-4

177 pp., 8x11, 60 illustrations $34.95. The only book specifically written for writers to sell television and feature film movie screenplays and theatrical stage plays to literary agents and production companies. Many books explain how to write scripts, but this one tells how to get them sold! Insider industry secrets of marketing scritps are revealed.

INTERNET ADDRESS BOOK WITH COMPUTER BACK UP FILES

ISBN-10: 0-916367-12-6 ISBN-13: 978-0-916367- 12-1

116 pp., 8x11, $19.95 Never lose another important password, ID number, e-mail or Internet contact. Log them here in this book. Also, enter your computer data files so you can recover from computer failure, theft, fire, flood, or just making a file deletion error.

AN EVENING OF COMEDY SKITS – 11 TEN MINUTE THEATRICAL PLAYS

ISBN-10: 0-916367-32-0 ISBN-13: 978-0-916367-32-9

117 pp., 8x11, $34.95. A collection of 11 ten minute comedy sketches. Plays are low budget with common household props and focusing on the funny relationships between men and women. Two parodies included of two TV shows: "Cops" and "The Dating Game. Suitable for general audiences.

STAGE PLAY – A COMEDY THEATRICAL PLAY

ISBN-10: 0-916367-34-7 ISBN-13: 978-0-916367- 34-3

132 pp., 8x11, $12.95 Two women must get married at all cost and they pick two goofy actors using every trick in the book to get the "I do". A fast-pace, low-budget, full-length comedy play focusing on the courtship ritual. No harsh offensive dialog. Common household props. Strong emotional acting.

TRUE BUMS - A COMEDY SCREENPLAY

ISBN-10: 0-916367-26-6 ISBN-13: 978-0-916367-26-8

118 pp., 8x11, $12.95. Three movie executives burned out on life escape the good life of Hollywood to become bobos on a California railroad. Here they discover other rich men doing the same, living the high-life in lavish Disneyland-like fantasy whistle stops, until the wives find out, steal a freight train and the great train chase is on. The bums must save Christmas at all costs from the wives who are determined to capture and return them home, forever!

REVENGE OF THE GRANNIES - A COMEDY SCREENPLAY

ISBN-10: 0-916367-25-8 ISBN-13: 978-0-916367-25-1

124 pp., 8x11, $12.95 Rich grandmothers fed up with crime and a corrupt mayor form a military assault team, MEBOM, to wage full-scale war against the city of Lost Angus street gangs and city hall. Military fireworks and destruction is severe, though nobody is killed in this comedy screenplay. Grandma is the hero!

WALKING WITH THE LORD A CHRISTIAN DEVOTIONAL – DAILY INSPIRATIONAL & WITNESSING INSTRUCTIONS

ISBN-10: 0-916367-19-3 ISBN-13: 978-0-916367-19-0

140 pp., 8x11, $12.95. A powerful daily devotional focusing on what a believer can do for the Lord with hundreds of instructions on how to prepare for God's service. Become a positive and effective witnesses to the Lord. Written for those who believe the Bible to bear good fruit.

HOW TO CHANGE THE OIL IN YOUR TWIN CAM HARLEY DAVIDSON MOTORCYCLE

ISBN-10: 0-916367-75-6 ISBN-13: 978-0-916367-75-6

136 pp., 5.5x8.5, $34.95 A guide on how to change the three oil compartments on the motorcycle. Also replacing the air filter and spark plugs with valuable engine longevity advice. Written for the rider who wants to learn how to do it himself. This book makes it easy to learn with 80 photographs and highly detailed step-by-step instructions.

THE OATMAN ARIZONA HOLY LAND TOUR

ISBN-10: 0-916367-17-7 ISBN-13: 978-0-916367-17-6

104 pp., 5.5x8.5, 60 photographs, $19.95 A Self-guided 60 mile automobile and motorcycle tour of Arizona rock formations resembling Biblical scenes near Oatman, Arizona. A new tourist attraction near Laughlin, Nevada. The tour is on Route 66 and entirely accessible by paved roads. No other tourist attraction in the USA has more Biblical rock formations than in Oatman, Arizona. The tour is on old Route 66.

BOOK ORDER FORM

QUANTITY TITLE RETAIL PRICE

___Steam & Diesel Power Plant Examinations $34.95 _______
___Trap Shooting Secrets $34.95 _______
___Precision Shooting - The Trapshooters Bible $34.95 ______
___Screen & Stage Marketing Secrets $34.95________
___Internet Address Book $12.95________
___An Evening of Comedy Skits $34.95________
___Walking With The Lord Christian Devotional $12.95________
___True Bums $12.95________
___Revenge of the Grannies $12.95________
___Stage Play $12.95________
___How to Change the Oil in Your Twin Cam Motorcycle - Harley Davidson $34.95
___The Oatman Arizona Holy Land Tour $19.95

Shipping: $4 per book. $6 for two books. ____________
Nevada business: Sales/Use Tax resale number # ____________
TOTAL: Shipping Charge and Purchase Price of Books $ ____________
Send order and payment to the mailing address listed on our Website.

BOOK TRADE SPECIAL ORDERS

PLEASE SEND A PURCHASE ORDER WITH YOUR SHIPPING ADDRESS, BILLING ADDRESS AND PURCHASE ORDER NUMBER.

TRADE DISCOUNT:
Bookstores 20% "Special Order" discount. Net/30
Wholesalers 37%. Terms Net/90. Distributors inquire.

PLEASE PURCHASE OUR BOOKS FROM OUR WHOLESALERS:
For Print on Demand books contact Lightning Source listed here.
Baker & Taylor: www.btol.com Phone 908-218-3950
Ingram: www.ingrambookgroup.com Phone 800-937-8000
Lightning Source USA www.lightningsource.com Phone 615-213-5815
Lightning Source UK www.lightningsource.co.uk Phone +44(0)1908 443555
Brodart Company: www.brodart.com Phone 800-233-8467
Spring Arbor also wholesales our Christian books. Phone 800-395-4340

HAVE YOU SEEN OUR ART GALLERY? VISIT OUR WEBSITE!

James Russell Publishing

James Russell, 205 Rainbow Drive, # 10585, Livingston, TX 77399
SAN 295-852X. Web site: JamesRussellPublishing.com

VISIT OUR WEBSITE FOR MORE BOOKS

FUN BOOK SERIES

JamesRussellPublishing.com

OATMAN ARIZONA HOLY LAND TOUR

See awesome and mysterious natural rock-art formations the next time you attend the Laughlin, Nevada Motorcycle Rally! It's all in the book.

AND

Check out our motorycle rally books that show you things you have never seen before! We also have free rally guide maps.

Come visit: JamesRussellPublishing.com

**MOTORCYCLE
&
AUTOMOBILE
SELF-GUIDED
TOURS!**

RIVER WALK TOUR

FREE SELF-GUIDED AT YOUR LIESURE **FREE**

SEE MYSTERIOUS NATURAL ART

ROCK FORMATIONS

Free - Self-guided Auto & Motorcycle Tour

N W E S

Start Here In Laughlin, NV

1. Go to the Riverside Casino south parking lot to begin the free Riverwalk tour.

2

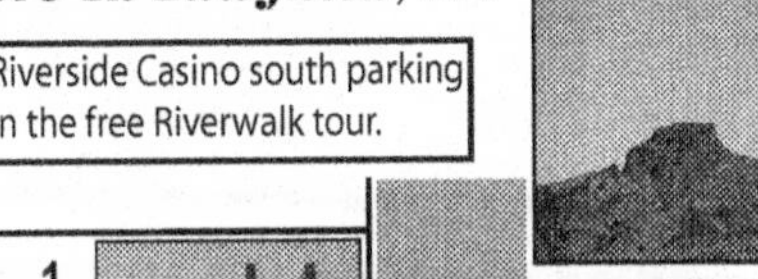

1.

South Parking Lot

BRING THE KIDS

Entrance

3

2. Look across the river to the far left to see Mr. Monkey. He's going to Vegas!

3. Gaze straight ahead (east) to see Sting Ray mountain. Notice the detail. It has eyes and even a grinning mouth!

4

4. To the right is the Wicked Witch of the West 's Castle.

5. Arizona's version of Wyoming's Devil's Tower.

5

6. Sleeping Woman. Her head is to the left as she gazes to heaven.

6

7. The Sea Serpent is the undulating rock formation from left to center.

7. The Sea Serpent is attacking the Pirate Ship in the distance as seen in the far right of the photograph. The ship lost its center mast from the Sea Serpent attack.

7

Riverwalk Sidewalk

COLORADO RIVER

Riverwalk Sidewalk

You have just learned a new talent by developing "artistic eyes" to recognize cleverly hidden rock art formations. How many more images can you find?

8 River Walk Tour Ends Here.

Continue to Oatman, AZ On Reverse Side

over

Visit: JamesRussellPublishing.com

ATTACH YOUR BUSINESS CARD BELOW

CPSIA information can be obtained at www.ICGtesting.com
Printed in the USA
BVOW08s1659080716

454598BV00001B/57/P